MW00337200

Endorsements for

The ABCs of Marriage
Building a Solid Foundation for Marital Success

by Tim Gustafson

"We have known Tim Gustafson for over 25 years and have personally seen him use these principles to help marriages. He and his wife, Reneé, have also worked at having a marriage that will last a lifetime. We believe that this book can be a very useful tool to help people gain a greater understanding regarding their marriage and how to make it more fulfilling. There is a great deal of practical wisdom to be found in the pages of *The ABCs of Marriage* and we highly recommend it."

— *Mike and Diane Bickle*
International House of Prayer, Kansas City

* * * * *

"Tim Gustafson's *The ABCs of Marriage* is an interactive, practical, wisdom-filled guide to building great marriages. It is also a wonderful counseling tool for pastors and lay leaders alike. I am recommending this book to all in my congregation, as well as all of the pastors and churches in our network!"

— *Howard Cordell, Pastor, Faith Covenant Church*
President, Midwest Ministers Fellowship

* * * * *

"Does your marriage need a tune-up? Do you need additional tools to aid your communication skills with your spouse? Then the remedy is sitting right in your hands! With wisdom, insight, and revelation, Tim Gustafson brings us a powerful new book, *The ABCs of Marriage: Building a Solid Foundation for Marital Success*. We joyfully recommend the contents and the spirit of this book. Read it, and let your relationship breathe once again!"

— James W. and Michal Ann Goll
Cofounders of the Encounters Network
and Authors of "The Lost Art of Intercession,"
"God Encounters" and "A Call to the Secret Place"

* * * * *

"This is an honest and realistic book on the triumphs and trials of married life. Even the best relationships often run into conflicts; discovering how to talk and resolve them in truth and humility is an art for every couple to discover. *The ABCs of Marriage* is practical, inspiring, and very encouraging. I highly recommend it!"

— Melody Green, President,
Last Days Ministries

The ABCs of Marriage

Building a Solid Foundation for Marital Success

TIM GUSTAFSON

www.gustafsonconsulting.org

ISBN: 1-58597-364-5

Library of Congress Control Number: 2005935021

PUBLISHING
4500 College Blvd.
Overland Park, KS 66211
1/888/888-7696
www.leatherspublishing.com

To Reneé, my beloved wife.

CONTENTS

ACKNOWLEDGMENTS ix

INTRODUCTION xi

PART I: EVALUATE –
DISCOVERY OF THE PAST, PRESENT, AND FUTURE 1
    Chapter 1: Marriage Today 3
    Chapter 2: Personal History 14
    Chapter 3: Building Blocks 22

PART II: EQUIP –
THE ABCs OF MARRIAGE 37
    A – Appreciate Your Spouse 39
    B – Believe the Best 43
    C – Confess When You Are Wrong 49
    D – Date One Another Continually 56
    E – Encourage One Another 61
    F – Faith Is Significant 64
    G – Gentleness Is Very Valuable 68
    H – Hardheadedness Is Not an Advantage 74
    I – Intimacy With Your Spouse Is Very Special 79
    J – Joking at Your Spouse's Expense Is Harmful 84
    K – Knowing Your Spouse's Needs Is Vital 87
    L – Listen Very Carefully 102
    M – Money Needs To Be Handled With Care 111
    N – No Threats or Manipulation 121
    O – Opinions Need To Be Shared With Care 125
    P – Parenting Is a Team Activity 132
    Q – Quickly Make Peace 142
    R – Relationships Need Clear Boundaries 145

S – Sex Is For Marriage 150

T – Trust Is a Foundational Principle 161

U – Understanding Leads To Love 166

V – Vacations Are Important 173

W – Weeds Can Kill a Garden 176

X – X-ray Vision Is Helpful 179

Y – You Think of Your Spouse First 182

Z – Zest Is Not Just a Bar of Soap 186

PART III: ENCOURAGE –
LOOKING TOWARD TOMORROW 189
   Making Your Marriage Last a Lifetime 191

ACKNOWLEDGMENTS

I want to first thank my wife, Reneé, for helping me develop this book. She is my best friend and I have been inspired by her love, wisdom and strength. Her love and support have helped me grow in my understanding of women.

I want to thank my three children, Tara, Amy and Joel, for their love, encouragement and affection. I am very proud of them and thank them for their support. I also want to thank their spouses, Jeff, Jason, and future spouse, Lindsay.

A special word of appreciation goes to Austin, Carson and Alexia, and to my future grandchildren. You are fabulous.

I want to thank my father and mother, Mervin and Evelyn Gustafson, for their loving efforts to teach me how to honor and love others. They also introduced me to Jesus, who has been my greatest source of help and strength. They have celebrated over 55 years of marriage and have passed the tests of time and built a marriage that has lasted a lifetime.

I thank my brother, Larry, his wife, Janie, and my sister, Pam. I have greatly appreciated their friendship and support through the years. I also want to thank Nancy Roberts, my mother-in-law, for her encouragement.

I thank Julie Hudspeth, who helped me with all her prayers, thoughts and reflections. I want to thank my friends, Steve and Jane Lambert, for reading the first draft and encouraging me to keep trying.

I thank the staff of Leathers Publishing, especially my editor, Mollie, who has been an encouragement to me and worked with me to produce a document that I am very proud of.

I thank my friends who have supported me and given me strength to finish this book, especially my small group and the "Power of a Praying Wife" group that prayed for me.

I also thank the many clients that have helped me learn how to build a foundation for marital success.

Finally, I give praise and thanks to God, because without His input, wisdom and encouragement, this book would have never been published.

INTRODUCTION

Imagine you are building a new house. You've dreamed, planned, and contemplated living in this place you will call home. It will have the floor plan, doors, windows, paint and landscaping you've desired. You are excited!

Well into the project you discover that although the wallpaper looks great, the foundation wasn't poured right, some of the wiring is missing and there is one room that will have no light fixture because you failed to include it in your plans. Then you find that some of the plumbing was not installed. There is no way to get clean water into the master bathroom, or get the sewage back out. You begin to realize your brand new home has some serious problems.

This house may have similarities to your marriage. Parts of it look great, but there are things that need to be changed, repaired or improved to make life more pleasant, more livable.

Many of my clients say their wedding day was the happiest day of their life. There were so many hopes and longings on the threshold of fulfillment. When they come into my office, the happy glow has slipped away or is painfully vacant.

This Book Is Designed To Help You:

- **Evaluate** your relationship – discovering where you are now, where you've been and where you hope to go.

- **Equip** you with tools – to help you and your husband or wife grow closer together and to help your marriage become stronger.

- **Encourage** you with expectations – of good things to come.

These "Three E's" will help you set the foundation right and show you how the wiring and plumbing of your marriage can be changed, replaced, upgraded and altered to turn your home into a place where peace and pleasure reign, where you are happy. They will be noted throughout the book.

Who Is This Book For?

- **Anyone who plans to marry.** You can help set yourself up for success.

- **Engaged couples.** Take a real-life approach to what's ahead and have fun in the discovery process.

- **Newlyweds.** Build your house right from the beginning.

- **Those who have "good" marriages.** You may be surprised, excited, and challenged to identify areas where you can make your relationship richer than you had previously dreamed. The icing on the cake can be even sweeter.

- **Those in marriages that are in trouble.** Life is worth fixing. Help is within your grasp.

I've Set the Book Up in Three Parts:

I. **Discovery of the Past, Present and Future** – Assessing where you are, realizing, in part, how you got there, and gathering how-to's on improving your marriage no matter how good or bad it is right now. *Evaluate.*

II. **The ABCs of Marriage** – Targeted important areas in marriage. A letter a day helps keep marriage difficulties away. *Equip.*

III. **Looking Toward Tomorrow** – You can live in a state of expecting good and knowing that when trouble arises, there are ways to come out on the other side waving a victory flag rather than a white flag of surrender and defeat. *Encourage.*

Read, learn, and step out of your old patterns or comfort zones. Endeavor to use these building blocks today, tomorrow, and for a lifetime.

The happiness, the enjoyment, the oneness you desire in marriage is attainable.

PART I – EVALUATE

Discovery of the
Past, Present, and Future

Chapter 1

MARRIAGE TODAY

"We were so in love," said Andy, as he sat on my couch that chilly winter day. "Jenny and I were so happy. Even after we got married, these feelings were alive. Now I sometimes look at her and think, 'Is this all there is?' "

When I asked Andy and Jenny about how they had met and how their romance developed, they perked up. Remembering those times brought smiles. Jenny's stiff posture relaxed. Andy turned toward Jenny. His look was soft. When the conversation got back to a problem area, the stiffness returned, and the smiles were gone.

Often when I have asked the question, "When did the romance stop?" I hear couples tell me, "It was in the first two or three years or the first weeks." I've even heard, "The first few days." It is not uncommon for them to tell me that their romance faded long before they came to see me. It may be helpful for you to know that the romance or "magic" often fades into the background or even totally disappears. In this book we will look at ways to recapture it.

Like the house described in the introduction, Andy and Jenny's marriage needed some changes if they were going to enjoy the contentment they were wanting.

Where Are You Today in Your Relationship with Your Spouse?
• Are you in love?
• Are you worn out?
• Is your heart dead toward your spouse?
• Are you somewhere in between?

A Look at Where We Are Going

One of the goals in this book is to give you tools that can help you improve your marriage. You don't use a wrench to put in a new light bulb; you simply use your hand. You don't use a needle to open a stopped up drain; you use a plunger. Having the appropriate tools can make all the difference.

I hope to take you through self-discovery regarding your relationship, help you open up, give you insights, target specific areas, give you several key ingredients for a successful marriage, and show you how to use them.

Reality/Truth Statements

I am going to include several written exercises that will make this book even more beneficial than just reading about how to improve your marriage. This is part of the **Discovery** process. Your responses will help you see where you've been, how you got where you are, and give you insights on how to satisfy your vision of a fulfilling marriage. Let's start with a little inventory. Look around you. *Your answers count.*

Note: When both husband and wife are doing the exercises, separate copies of the book offer each person more freedom in answering.

Evaluate: What Do You Need?

Let's do an inspection of your marriage, a check-up if you will. You check and refill the fluids in your car. You keep putting in fuel. You have repairs done to keep it running well. It is the same with your marriage. Ask yourself these questions. Take time in answering and write them down. We will do several of these evaluations in Part I.

1) What do you need to help your marriage be more fulfilling?

    a. _____

    b. _____

    c. _____

2) What do you hope to gain from reading this book?

   a. _____

   b. _____

   c. _____

3) What are the three greatest strengths in your marriage?

   a. _____

   b. _____

   c. _____

4) What are the three areas that need the most help?

   a. _____

   b. _____

   c. _____

The sub-title of this book is *Building a Solid Foundation for Marital Success.* This book will help you discover whether or not you are nurturing your spouse and your relationship and building the foundation to give you success in your marriage.

If you believe that you have a pretty good marriage, stop and think for a moment where it can be improved. Some of these areas of improvement might be the things you wrote down in #4 above. As you think this over, remember it is so easy to look for ways that your spouse needs to change. Rather than changing your spouse, consider the areas of your behavior that you can alter or modify.

Filling in the blanks of the questions above, and the ones to follow, is an important step in taking responsibility for your own part in the changing and building process.

Mirror, Mirror on the Wall

Go look in a mirror. Who do you see? The one you see is the one who is reading this book. It is the one who has the power to choose to make things better. The person you see when you look in the mirror can be a hero. Remember that as you read this book, take time to think, answer the questions and seek solutions.

Marriage Today

Marriage is not a dying institution. It is a changing one. More people than ever continue to get married. However, more people divorce than ever before — not because divorce is easier, but because people expect so much more out of marriage. About half of all marriages will probably end in divorce, and first marriages will last an average of eight years.

The Challenge to Marriage

The institution of marriage is being challenged today on many different fronts. Divorce, family desertion, wife battering, child abuse, youth delinquency, marital boredom, emotional pain, living together and unhappiness make marriage often a very damaging experience. Sometimes there is the desire to just get away from it all and go live in a cave, alone, far away from kids, spouses, family, and even friends. However, living an isolated life is not the answer.

Just Like a Rock

Years ago, Paul Simon wrote a song, "I Am A Rock." In it he describes a person being like an island, isolated, alone — someone who has built lots of walls and doesn't let anyone enter into their world. This person has numbed himself so completely that he feels no pain and is isolated from himself and others.

No one can develop freely in this world and find a full life without feeling understood by at least one person. We need community, people around us to help us keep perspective regarding ourselves and others.

You cannot live in a marriage for long without realizing that living life as a rock is not going to work. Marriage challenges the very core of a person trying to live an independent life. Marriage is about being *interdependent* with another person.

6

Changes Are Often Difficult

There have been profound changes in women's and men's roles, relationships and identities within the last two decades. The rising consciousness and appropriate insistence of women that they have fair, equal opportunities to develop and use their full potential in careers and in homemaking, and participate equally in the decision-making of a family still threatens many men.

The young couples that I sit with in my office are often blurring the traditional roles of the 1950s and '60s. These young couples share grocery shopping, washing, cleaning, caring for the children, paying the bills, and even mowing the lawn. They watched their parents choose different roles and are opting for living their own lifestyle.

The fact that it sometimes takes two incomes to survive financially has forced many couples to share the responsibilities of managing a home even if they really don't want to.

Two-Career Marriages

More and more couples are facing the complexities and pressures of two-career marriages. It has been my experience when both spouses have jobs, there is increased stress and tension in their marriage and in their home, especially if there are children in the family.

Even if one spouse works full-time and one works part-time, both spouses working can complicate things. These marriages are often more prone to conflict and frustration than when there is only one person working full-time.

Remarriage and Step-Parenting

Remarriage and step-parenting are also current major American lifestyles. This adds to the difficulty of having a fulfilled marriage. Parenting is challenging enough when you have raised your children from birth. Step-parenting adds another challenge. When families become more disconnected, there is also a continuing decline in the support available to couples from their extended families.

Different Than What We Imagined

When Carly Simon reflected on marriage in her song, "That's the

Way I've Always Heard It Should Be," she illustrated a marriage that is far from what a healthy marriage is to look like. She told of a lack of communication, a couple living very separate lives, not being in touch with their children's needs, hating themselves for what they are and therefore hating one another.

Many get married thinking the marriage experience is going to be quite different than what it actually ends up being. The ABCs in this book are specific keys that will help you live a different life than the one found in Carly Simon's song.

Current Marriage Mindsets

This is a brief list of some of the current ideas that I have found among my clients regarding marriage:

• Don't marry until you can be sure you will have your own money, your own assets, your own profession and your own circle of friends.

• The purpose of marriage is to be happy.

• If it doesn't work out the first time, I'll just try again.

• Why not just live together? It is a lot easier, and if it doesn't work out, it won't be so painful. It will make being married better. Statistics reveal that neither of these is true.

It is obvious from these descriptions of marriage mindsets that there needs to be a clearer picture painted of what a marriage is really all about.

Most people that I have met with over the years want their marriage to be a lifelong partnership. However, after the wedding day vows and as the marriage begins to get more and more difficult, the reality causes many to reconsider their commitment.

Where are you? Did you plan on your marriage lasting a lifetime? Are you willing to undergo some changes so it will?

Marriage Is a Mystery

Marriage is not a simple thing to understand. It is a mystery of unfolding truth. You will continue to keep learning about marriage, a little at a time, throughout your life.

Marriage has been evaluated and studied from almost every angle. However, it is still hard to explain what happens between a man and woman when they fall in love. Marriage is romantic and almost too realistic. It is solemn and yet joyful. It gives the opportunity for every type of emotion to be present. Often these different expressions occur in a matter of a few minutes, making one feel as if they are continually caught off guard.

Evaluate: Where You Were

Why did you marry your spouse? What was it that captured you about them? Take a moment and write your answer.

_____

_____

_____

_____

_____

_____

I Have Heard All Kinds of Answers to This Question

I don't know. I can't remember. I was in love. They were so good-looking. They were so kind. I was convinced they were the right one for me. It just happened. God told me they were the one. My folks felt it would be a good idea. I wanted out of my home and they took me away.

Remembering why you married has a twofold purpose:

1) It might help to relight the flames of passion.
2) It might help you identify several of the problems that have made being married difficult.

In the discovery process it is important to try to make sense of your past history. Recalling why you wanted to get married will help you figure out what needs to be done to improve your situation.

So you got married for whatever reason, the task at hand is greater than just staying together. It is making your marriage work, finding peace, having it be a vital source of fulfillment and satisfaction for you and your spouse.

A Great Payoff

As formidable a task as it might seem to have a solid marriage, the payoff is great. The human soul has a wonderful opportunity for fulfillment.

Evaluate: Where You Are Right Now

Pick up your pen, write your answers to the following questions. You may discover things you had not previously realized.

1) When you talk, are you merely saying words to each other. Or are you actually conversing, consciously and carefully listening to one another?

_____

_____

2) Do you really care how your spouse feels? Or are you just saying what you think to get it off your chest or to let your opinion be known?

_____

_____

3) When you talk to your partner, do they know you are trying to express what is in your heart and mind? _____

4) Has your love grown cold for your partner? _____

5) Is your marriage still enjoyable? _____

6) Was your marriage ever enjoyable? _____

7) How are you expressing your love for your partner?

_____

_____

8) When you are expressing your love for your partner, do they know that you are showing love to them? Do they recognize it?

_____

_____

_____

9) What does he/she do that makes you smile?

_____

_____ .

10) Are you complimenting them and thanking them for doing these things?

_____

11) What do you do that makes him/her smile?

_____

_____ .

12) Have your spouse answer this question, "I feel more like loving you when you:

_____ ."

Work as a Team

If you feel your marriage is just fine, take a chance and ask your spouse what he or she thinks. They may have a different perspective than yours.

There does not have to be something wrong with your marriage for you to make it better. For example, if you are enjoying a date night, a step-up could mean enjoying it more. You might talk about different places you would like to go, or exploring new things you want to experience together.

This Will Help

The ABCs will help you begin to supply the nourishment and the ingredients that can strengthen your marriage. If you are feeling discouraged, you might wonder if it can ever get better. I want to provide you with some practical principles that will help get you out of a current trouble spot. Knowing these tools are available can give you something to reach for in difficult times by showing how to work through your difficulties and come out stronger. I encourage you to practice the principles you learn until they are a natural part of the way you love your spouse. What is practice? It is doing something over and over until it is a normal behavior.

A Healthy Relationship

Having a healthy marriage doesn't just happen. It takes desire and some serious effort. A fulfilling marriage is attainable; it is within your reach. I will be identifying some **marriage builders** which strengthen a marriage and **marriage killers** which bring quick ruin to a relationship. Most of these builders and killers will be easily noticed. You can eliminate the killers and use suggested tools and techniques to help you have a marriage that will last a lifetime.

Struggling Along

Most people have never had anyone help them understand the basics of a healthy relationship. They received very little instruction regarding how to nurture a marriage and help it to be fulfilling. They just struggle along doing what they think is best, using what they learned from watching their parents.

They live the same way their parents lived, acting just as their parents acted. They don't know anything different. They have never seen another model. This often leads to a great deal of frustration.

Frustration! What Do You Do?

It is very common for me to sit with men, young and old, who have never had another man help them learn how to understand their wives. Many men don't know whom to ask for guidance or don't even know they need help. They are often too proud or afraid to ask another man for advise, often feeling they will be judged. Men easily become defensive and hesitant to open up and seek support or encouragement.

Many women who sit in my office have grown up in a home where men were not honored or respected, often for good reasons. Their friends have lousy marriages and let them know it. Why should they experience anything different? They watched their moms live through frustrating marriages and seldom heard anything good about men. The old saying, "You can't live with them and you can't live without them," is totally true to these women.

So, Where Do You Learn How To Do Marriage?

The best place for a man or woman to learn how to love and understand each other is in their home, being instructed by a wise, loving, caring father and mother. This seldom happens. Since there is so little opportunity to learn about marriage, young men grow up without positive models and settle for far less than they could experience by applying a few basic principles. Young women grow up longing for intimacy and for their "Prince Charming" to romance and pursue them and take them away. They often find little romance and end up being the one who pursues their man.

As you continue to evaluate your marriage, it is important to understand your family of origin. In Chapter 2, I will help you understand what you learned from your parents and how they impacted you.

Chapter 2

PERSONAL HISTORY

My Parents

Growing up, I experienced a home where the marriage vow was respected. My mom and dad have been married over fifty years. I watched my dad love my mom, and I saw my mom honor and respect my dad. In our home there were the normal struggles that accompany family life; however, I didn't have to live through divorce, violence, abuse, or alcoholism. This has helped me have a perspective of marriage that is much more positive than many of the people who sit in my office.

I am very realistic about the difficulty of making a marriage work, and yet hopefully you will sense my belief that it can be wonderfully enjoyable and fulfilling.

My Wife

I met Reneé in college. One evening I asked her to go out with me to get some ice cream. We talked and talked late into the night. She was like no other woman I had ever known. She was a great listener. We began to spend a good deal of time together. Friendship turned to romance. My love and interest for her increased daily. Finally, I knew I wanted to marry her.

Soon we faced a problem. I wanted to have a dozen children, and she didn't know if she even wanted any. I wanted my wife to stay at home, wait on me hand and foot, cook all my meals, clean my house, wash my clothes, and even iron my underwear.

I wanted her to be just like my mom. She, interestingly enough, wanted a husband who would cook and clean and even do the wash. I knew I loved her, but I wasn't sure I could give up my dream woman. Obviously, we had plenty of room for discussion.

In spite of this seven-foot hurdle in front of us, we were fixed on problem-solving, not on letting the problems divide us. After compromising and deciding that we would both help with the responsibilities of the home, we also agreed to wait and see regarding children.

It was obvious to me that she was the woman for me. I was willing to change my expectations and so was she. I proposed and eighteen months later we were married.

Did It Work?

Even though it has been challenging, we have experienced joy, companionship, romance, and intimacy throughout our marriage. We have three grown children and grandchildren. We have faced the normal challenges of raising children, along with experiencing the fun and enjoyment that they bring.

Yes, we have disagreements. Yes, we get frustrated, but we also press forward and choose to find workable answers. We have learned to agree to disagree and still honor, love, and respect one another without yelling, screaming, or being violent. I will say more about this under letter G, when I talk about healthy arguing.

We continue to look straight at the problems and not run from them. We are jumping the hurdles. The very things that have helped us and other couples stay in the race are in this book. Yes, we bloodied a knee here and there when we stumbled and fell, but we got up and kept going.

It's a Process

It's a process, like life itself; it takes time, desire, and determination to pass through the hard times. You can choose to work through difficulties and differences.

During their marriage a couple learns what works and what doesn't work, often through very painful trial and error periods.

Many people rarely figure out a better way of handling certain situations in their marriage. They just "muddle through," ending up with a great deal of frustration. For most couples, this is not the best. It doesn't strengthen a marriage or give them success.

Sometimes they go see a counselor or just decide to quit and get divorced. Maybe they will try marriage again, hoping it will be different the next time. But will it?

I'm going to tell you real-life ideas to help you learn how to make your marriage better. If things are going pretty well, my desire is to aid you in fine-tuning your marriage skills. Either way, I want to help.

Evaluate: Your Role Models

Let's start where you started. Consider your parents. Answer these questions. Written responses will give you stronger insights than passing thoughts. Be proactive here.

Your Father

Describe your father's relationship to your mother:

_____

_____

_____.

How did he treat her?

_____

_____

_____.

Did he yell at her, order her around, demean her, demand things from her?

_____.

Was he kind to her, gentle with her? Did he serve her, honor her? Did he encourage her, partner with her, ask her what she wanted?

_____

_____.

A good indicator of how you learned to respond to women hinges on how your father, or significant male role model, responded to your mother or women in general. Your attitude toward women and men has been influenced significantly by watching your father and mother interact.

Your Mother

Describe your mother's relationship to your father.

_____

_____.

How did she treat him?

_____

_____

_____.

Did she yell at him, order him around, demean him, demand things from him?

_____

_____.

Was she respectful to him, gentle, speaking encouraging words to him, supporting him? Did she serve him, speak well of him, honor him? Did she love him and show it? How did she show it?

_____

_____.

A good indicator of how you learned to respond to men hinges on how your mother, or significant female role model while you were growing up, responded to your father or men in general. You also learned how to relate to women by watching how she interacted with other women.

Parents

For many men and women, the tragedy of the day is that their parents were absent. Often, what a young boy or girl learned was that parents weren't really an honored, important part of the family. There is a longing in the hearts of these people for a relationship with a mom or dad, especially if they have not had that growing up.

If mom was a very needy woman or a very controlling woman, you may have a negative view of women. If she was self-confident and able to trust your father as he exercised his leadership, then you will probably feel more favorably toward women.

If your father was a demanding, demeaning, controlling, angry man, your view of men in general might be quite negative. However, if your father was a kind, soft, gentle, loving person you will most likely view men as a place of refuge and safety.

What you observed in your home as you watched your mother and father relate to each other has impacted you and may be a significant part of the struggles you are experiencing in your marriage. Understanding this is an important part of the continuing **Discovery** process.

Nobody

Nobody had a perfect model to follow. Nobody. If you had a good one, you have more from which to draw. If recalling your past feels dark or painful, you can choose to walk out your marriage in a better direction. You can create a new legacy. Many others have done it before you. You can do it, too.

A Re-cap

Okay, we're through with our evaluation for the moment. Here is a review of the questions that you have answered so far. Take a moment and review them.

- What do you need to help your marriage be more fulfilling?
- What do you hope to gain from reading this book?

- What are the three greatest strengths in your marriage?
- What are the three areas that need help the most?
- When you talk are you merely saying words to each other?
- Are you actually conversing, consciously and carefully listening to one another?
- Do you really care how your spouse feels? Or are you just saying what you think to get it off your chest or to let your opinion be known?
- When you talk to your partner, do they know you are trying to express what is in your heart and mind?
- Has your love grown cold for your partner?
- Is your marriage still enjoyable? Was it ever enjoyable?
- How are you expressing your love for your partner?
- When you are expressing your love for your partner, do they know that you are showing love to them? Do they recognize it?
- What does he/she do that makes you smile?
- Are you complimenting them and thanking them for doing these things?
- What do you do that makes him/her smile?
- Describe your father's relationship to your mother.
- How did he treat her? Did he yell at her, order her around, demean her, demand things from her?
- Was he kind to her, gentle with her? Did he serve her, honor her?
- Did he encourage her, partner with her, ask her what she wanted?
- Describe your mother's relationship to your father.
- How did she treat him? Did she yell at him, order him around, demean him, demand things from him? Was she respectful to him, gentle, speaking encouraging words to him, supporting him? Did she serve him, speak well of him, honor him? Did she love him and show it? How did she show it?

I will continue to ask you questions which will enable you to more correctly evaluate how your marriage is doing and whether it is on course to last a lifetime. But for the moment, are you in need of some fine-tuning, or a major overhaul?

The Desire Is There

Most men I meet have a great desire to learn how to love their wives.

They have rarely had anyone help them. Likewise, most women I meet long to know how to honor, love, and respect their husbands. They have had few real-life learning experiences watching this modeled for them.

The ABCs are proven to work. I've shared these principles for years. Those who embrace them and use them get results.

Life Is Often Just Hard

Today many husbands and wives are exhausted just trying to meet the responsibilities that are accompanied with family, work, church, community, parents, friends, and neighbors. The fast-paced society and the overload of information also contributes to the current situation of feeling overwhelmed with life. Many marriages would be in better shape if more time was simply allotted to working together, being together, and working as a team.

Appearances, Appearances

It is not uncommon for a couple to look good on the outside, but their marriage is passionless. The outward appearance is deceiving. Maybe yours is the same way. Perhaps this is how your parents lived.

Your marriage can improve. The cycle of boredom, emptiness, anger and fear does not have to be your experience.

If your marriage is to grow, it will require some honest assessment. Celebrate the places where it is working and identify the areas that need help. When you discover the areas that need help, it is necessary to begin to partner together with your spouse to make them better.

Partnership is a key.

Moving Forward

You can have a marriage that not only looks good in public, but also reflects what you are living at home.

You may be reading this book with a sense of disappointment or sadness regarding your marriage. You may have a glimmer of hope trying to figure out how you can help it be more fulfilling and meaningful. This is the place to begin. Having a willingness to carefully consider what needs to change in your marriage and how you can help accomplish it is the first step.

The Bible says that "without a vision people perish." One of my goals for you is that you can catch a vision of what a marriage that will last a lifetime looks like.

In the next chapter I am going to help you see the vision even more clearly and hopefully help you realize that it is possible for you to experience this in your own life.

Chapter 3

BUILDING BLOCKS

Here come the trucks to deliver materials for building your dream home. Chapter 3 will open your eyes to see what some of these materials are.

Three Spheres That Have the Potential To Change Your Life

Getting the Picture

Let's put some guidelines to what a fulfilling, nurtured marriage looks like. There are Three Spheres in a marriage that we will be looking at. They are:

> **Sphere 1: Relational** fulfillment with your spouse.
> **Sphere 2: Financial** fulfillment.
> **Sphere 3: Family and Friend** fulfillment.

- **Sphere 1:** Involves the spheres of communication, conflict resolution, intimacy, sexuality, and expectations.

- **Sphere 2:** Can best be evaluated by asking some questions. Is there peace or conflict regarding money in your home? Are you able to pay your bills? Are you as debt-free as you can be? Are you living within your means? Are you using a budget? And is it working?

- **Sphere 3:** Involves other relationships, your interaction with your children, in-laws, and friends.

These Spheres are here to help you evaluate, consider and improve your marriage. If you are experiencing fulfillment in them, there will be well-being, and contentment in your home. If this is true, you are doing a good job of nurturing your marriage. Ahead, we will look at each one of these areas in greater detail.

Evaluate: How Are You Doing?

Fill in a quick evaluation of your marriage using the numbers listed below. Write a number between 1-10 in the blank, such as, **1 – not doing very well; 5 – doing okay; 10 – doing great.**

Sphere 1:

____ Communication

____ Conflict resolution

____ Intimacy

____ Sexuality

____ Your personal expectations being met

Sphere 2:

____ Contentment regarding your finances

____ Able to pay your bills

____ Debt-free as you can be

____ Living within your means

____ Using a budget

Sphere 3:

____ Relationships with your children

____ Relationships with your in-laws

____ Relationships with your friends

What To Do Next

If at all possible, have your spouse also do an evaluation. Share your answers with each other and then compare them. Work together.

If your scores are not as high as you want them to be, don't get overwhelmed and quit. Rather, let this brief survey challenge you to figure out how to raise your score.

Find the areas that are 5 or less and start by focusing there. Remember, you're looking for places where you can change for the better, not where you can find fault with your mate or make him/her change. Start with just one area in order that you don't get overwhelmed and quit.

The Most "Bang" for Your Buck

In which of these three spheres is the most crucial need? _____

_____

Where could you get the greatest return in the shortest amount of time?

_____

Not feeling fulfilled in any of the three spheres of life is extremely costly. It's time to bring a greater measure of nurture and fulfillment in your home. Begin putting the wiring in where it is missing and add the proper plumbing to the master bathroom.

A House Fire

If your home is on fire, the firemen will rush into your living room and put out the burning curtains before they address the candle on the coffee table that started it. The most threatening places must be dealt with first. The same is true of your marriage. Let's identify the greatest needs and those that have the greatest potential for disaster. After they are identified, you can begin to bring change to them.

I've prepared this book in such a way for you to go through the ABCs and find a few subjects that you might want to focus on more than others. The scores and questions which you have already answered will help guide you.

You may not want to begin with the toughest letter first. Choose one that is doable. Face the problem, get ready for hurdles, and look ahead to winning.

Putting the Plan into Action

When my wife and I were first married, we discovered that if we talked about finances before bed, we often ended up in a negative conversation. I didn't know about these three spheres then, but if I had, I would have recognized that we had a problem with **Sphere 1**, communication, and also **Sphere 2**, finances.

We first addressed the **Sphere 1** communication problem and agreed that we would not go to bed thinking and talking about financial concerns. We were too tired at this time to have a meaningful conversation without getting angry with each other. We later addressed **Sphere 2**. That was many years ago, and we still practice this to help us reach our goal and win, instead of losing.

We Are All Learning

Very few people have all three spheres in their marriage running smoothly at the same time. A couple might get finances right for a while, but miss on intimacy. They might get communication right, but miss with their friends and family.

Don't Settle for Mediocrity

You may feel that things are working smoothly. Check with your spouse. They will confirm or call into question your perspective. If you feel like you are doing "okay" in your marriage, you might consider raising the bar, challenging yourself with higher standards. This will enable you to continue to grow.

Throughout your marriage, you will go in and out of feeling fulfilled in one way or another. That is the nature of life and of marriage. It is possible to experience both ongoing peace and a sense of well-being at the same time. Understanding these spheres will be helpful.

Four Major Components

Just as there are **Three Spheres** that give us a clearer picture of marriage, there are also **Four Major Components** in all marriages. These components are the **foundation** of a healthy marriage. If they are present, it will benefit your marriage. These components may occur simultaneously or one at a time. During difficult times, it may seem like not even one of them is present. They are:

1. **Passion and Romance**
2. **Companionship**
3. **Intimacy**
4. **Covenant and Commitment**

PASSION AND ROMANCE

It is often hard to explain why it happens. Those who have experienced it know that there is nothing like it. Passion keeps the heart working overtime. It is frequently characterized by the phrase, "you really turn me on!" It is often a sensual form of love that produces ardent physical involvement before and during marriage. If it exists without genuine love, what results is lust. Lust is using someone else for your own pleasure without thinking about what they want and need long term.

Many people have mistaken lust for love. Lust is when you want someone in a way that is not real love. It is passion separated from love. **Genuine love is willing to sacrifice what you want for the other person's betterment.**

Unrealistic – Nearly Insane

Many couples that I sit with are longing for passion to return or even begin in their marriage. It is possible for this to happen.

One of the greatest favors you will ever do for yourself is to settle it in your mind and heart that to live in the passion state perpetually is not only unrealistic but nearly insane.

The human body could not sustain the adrenaline flow. You would lose focus at work. Everyday chores and responsibilities wouldn't get done. Other friends and family members would be left out.

Many automobiles have a gauge on the dash that indicates how many RPMs the engine is running. RPMs means revolutions per minute. There is a red-line on the gauge that you are not to exceed. Your car is built to run below the red line most of the time. Sometimes it will exceed the line; however, if you ran it at, or above, the red line for long, you would quickly burn up your engine. Passion is much the same way.

The passion component is meant to be intermingled with companionship, intimacy and commitment. They all work together to make a healthy marriage.

COMPANIONSHIP

In a relationship, passion usually appears first. It is followed by companionship. When companionship comes first, the marriage is often stronger, because it is rooted in friendship and relationship. Companionship is the "I like you" feelings that stimulate all five senses. They smell good, they feel good, they sound good, they look good, and they are good company. This component is very important for marriages that last a lifetime.

However, if we base our love only on changeable characteristics we find attractive on the companionship level, when these things change, our feelings grow colder and colder until we wonder what we liked about our mates in the first place. Sometimes companionship cannot withstand the pressure of time. We all change. We don't smell as good, we don't look as good, we aren't such good company, and we don't sound that good.

INTIMACY

Intimacy usually comes after passion and companionship. It is when you are accepted by your partner for who you are. It is when you can have gut-level honesty and are safe to bare your soul. You are connected to your spouse in a way that no one else is. It is a place of safety, security, honesty and openness. I will say more about this later under the letter "I" – Intimacy.

COVENANT AND COMMITMENT

This is usually the last of the four, and yet hopefully it endures all the days that you and your spouse are alive. Commitment says things like, "I have searched my heart and I am willing to go through the hard times, through the times when I feel empty, and through the times when my romantic feelings are void. I will stay. I will seek answers and solutions when most of what is before me is problems. I will make challenging choices to not quit, knowing there will yet be better times when we are on the other side of this situation."

So What Does Your Marriage Look Like?

At this time you might say, "Passion has never been better in my marriage." Or you may wonder where the passion went. Passion is often the first of the four to fade in a marriage.

You might say, "Companionship has been great in my marriage." Or, you might wonder if you will ever be friends with your spouse again.

Some of you reading this book may be satisfied with the level of intimacy in your marriage, and yet others of you want more.

Some have made a conscious commitment to stay married, while others stay together out of habit, fear of the unknown, or have no place else to go.

You will go in and out of these four components throughout your marriage. You might not have had all of them present when you got married. Perhaps you've never had them all present at the same time. I want you to know it is possible.

One Is Better than None

You are probably reading this book because you have a desire to keep your commitment. If that is all that is keeping you in your marriage, when you would really rather just quit, I say, **"Way to go, Good Job!"** Don't give up just yet.

It is my hope that reading this book and actively walking-out the principles in it will give you more wisdom and understanding to help you increase passion, companionship, and intimacy. There is so much more for you.

Taking Time To Consider the Pain

If you are going to help your marriage become healthier, you will need to consider the areas in your marriage that cause you pain. I will give you opportunities to identify those places that have been unhealthy. It may benefit you to get help from a counselor.

The Wall of Protection

Consider your marriage like a wall protecting you. Let's identify the places in the wall that are already strong, the spots where there is deterioration, and the places that have crumbled and need to be rebuilt. There is also rubble here and there that must be cleared away. We want to identify ways you can be responsible for the areas that need rebuilding or repair. We will look for specific things you and your spouse can do which will make your marriage more fulfilling.

You can go into a dark closet and not find what you need until the light is switched on. The ABCs will turn on the light to help you see. Knowing specific things to do will give you hope.

Four Basic Actions

I have been working with married couples for over 25 years. One of the things I have learned is that many people who come to me just need encouragement and some basic advice. Many do things that are not beneficial, sometimes even harmful – and they aren't even aware of it. This may be true for you, too.

I have identified four basic actions, which, if you choose to begin to walk them out consistently, you will find your marriage growing stronger and stronger. They are:

1. **Taking Responsibility**
2. **Saying You're Sorry**
3. **Asking For, Receiving and Giving Forgiveness**
4. **Being Kind**

TAKING RESPONSIBILITY

Remember the person in the mirror? When you are willing to take responsibility in a situation, you identify that the problem was either created or intensified by your behavior.

Too often in our society the emphasis is upon finding someone to blame so we don't have to be responsible. In marriage, blaming the other person almost always increases the difficulty.

SAYING YOU'RE SORRY

Some ideas in this book will probably bring confrontation into your marriage. You may discover things about yourself and your marriage that you had not addressed or admitted to before. There will be opportunities for you to face your own mistakes. You may sense or realize the need to say, "I am sorry," or, "I have not done such and such the right way." When you say I'm sorry, you recognize your part in the conflict and give your partner hope that you might begin to understand why they are so offended. Saying and hearing this phrase can bring healing to your marriage.

ASKING FOR, RECEIVING AND GIVING FORGIVENESS

To some of you, the word "forgiveness" may merely be semantics. You may think it is the same as saying you are sorry. Asking for forgiveness is a necessary next step. It is stronger than just saying I'm sorry. It can wash a lot of dirt off the situation.

The difference between saying "I'm sorry" and "will you forgive me" is that "will you forgive me" gives your spouse the opportunity to respond to you. They will hopefully forgive you and let it go. If they choose not to, they face the prospect of living with an increasing bitterness in their heart toward you.

When a person harbors bitterness in their heart, it is like putting paper towels down their bathroom toilet. Eventually they will have to deal with the problem of sewage backing up in their home. Bitterness will eventually influence everything negatively.

When one person starts recognizing his/her error and asks for forgiveness, often it softens the spouse's heart and causes healing to flow. When you ask for and give forgiveness, you are planting seeds for your marriage to recover.

BEING KIND

The key ingredient underscoring all of the ABCs is *kindness*. This is huge. It is often described as being loving, affectionate, agreeable, or having a pleasant nature. It is one of those words that does not need a great deal of explanation. We instinctively understand it.

There are countless pictures in our everyday world that illustrate kindness. There is the person bagging your groceries at the corner store who is willing to carry those bags out to the car in the rain, even though it isn't really part of their job. Driving down the freeway, you see a person helping another change a flat tire. You recall a school teacher taking extra time helping you solve your math problems. When you see a mother looking at her children and saying, "Be kind," they seem to know what that means. You visualize the little mouse pulling the thorn out of the lion's paw in *Aesop's Fable*. You remember Dorothy befriending the scarecrow in the *Wizard of Oz*.

Marriage presents many opportunities for kindness. For example, you and your wife are sitting on the couch watching your favorite TV program, and she mentions that she is thirsty. You get up and get her a glass of water. That is kindness.

Your husband is exhausted from his day at the office and you take the children outside to play for a while, in order that he can have a few minutes of solitude to get refreshed for the rest of the evening. That is kindness.

You pick up your own dishes and put them in the dishwasher, even though you don't think it is your job. That is kindness.

These are just a few examples where you can *be kind* to your spouse and your family throughout each day.

Sometimes Kindness Is Hard

What makes being kind so difficult? Most of us don't like making sacrifices. Being kind often means that you will be inconvenienced. If you are one who is selfish, being kind will be difficult at first. Kindness involves giving up what you want or what you think you deserve.

If you become aware that you are not being a kind, thoughtful, considerate person and you are looking for ways to improve your marriage, this could be an open door to positive changes. You can be part of the answer. Take six months, nine months, a year to establish this new way of living. There are fabulous rewards for being kind. You'll see the soft smiles of those you treat well. You can change the lives of others for the better.

Watch your spouse's response. Watch your children, your neighbors, your co-workers. You will be amazed. The deeds start piling up. The memory of kindness will continue on and on. It imprints the hearts of those around you. You start feeling better as well. Kindness can cause the mistrust, anger, and misunderstandings in your marriage to disappear.

Most of us have already had enough meanness and inconsideration to last for the rest of our lives.

Evaluate: Kindness

List several ways you have been kind to your spouse in the last seven days.

a. _____

b. _____

c. _____

d. _____

Now list several ways in which you have experienced your spouse being kind to you in the last seven days. If you can't think of any, you can be the one to be a living example. You can be the one to turn the tide.

a. _____

b. _____

c. _____

d. _____

Finally identify several new ways in which you can begin to show kindness to your spouse. If you have trouble thinking of ways, ask them. Write them down.

a. _____

b. _____

c. _____

d. _____

Andy and Jenny

Remember Andy and Jenny? They wondered what had happened to their marriage.

They began to go through the ***Discovery*** process by identifying what they needed and wanted in their marriage in order for it to improve. They then made a list of what they needed and wanted and shared it with each other. They considered their past and began to uncover how they had become so disconnected from each other when they had been so "in love."

I introduced them to the basic ABCs, and a few meetings later they began to implement several of them. They discovered as they implemented them their marriage began to get stronger.

They became aware of the **Three Spheres:** relational, financial, and family and friend fulfillment. They recognized the strength and weaknesses of their **Major Components:** passion and romance, companionship, intimacy, covenant and commitment. They began to put into practice **The Basic Actions** in their marriage by taking responsibility for their own actions; recognizing those areas where they had hurt one another; telling each other they were sorry; asking for, receiving, and giving forgiveness; and acting with kindness toward each other. Their hope grew to begin to build and nurture their marriage.

They began to recognize places where they were continually hurting one another and began to work at changing those behaviors. Finally they wrote out some plans to work on and make it happen. They spent several months coming to my office and purposed to work on their relationship.

"Many times I have felt like quitting," Jenny told me in one session. Andy nodded. "Me, too," he said, "It just plain hurts to work through some of our problems. It's not been easy. I know I can't quit, but I want to."

Eventually the romantic feelings they had for each other began to return. It is still a struggle for them sometimes; they are still in process. It doesn't always work out that a couple has such success. But they are well on their way to a healthier relationship.

Is It Really Possible?

Having a marriage that is fulfilling to both husband and wife is not supposed to be as difficult as it has become. Have you ever heard the phrase, "As simple as ABC"?

Wouldn't it be something if there were some very basic principles of marriage that a person could learn that would help them have a more fulfilling marriage?

Learning How To Read

A child begins to learn how to read by first learning the building blocks of reading. If English is their language, they are taught the ABCs, the alphabet.

As a child you probably sang the ABC song. You may still sing it to your children or grandchildren.

A child learns the letters, then the sounds the letters make. They link the sounds together to form words. Words are joined to make sentences and paragraphs becoming complete expressions of thought.

The ABCs are like the foundation upon which a house is built. They will help you learn how to nurture and strengthen your marriage.

What You Have Been Given So Far

You've looked at why you got married and where you are now. There were blanks for you to fill in to show you whether or not you are expressing love to your spouse in ways he/she knows that they are being loved.

You've done some examination and evaluation of your own past life and family to give you some insights as to where you might be headed if you do not consciously decide where you want to go and how you will get there.

I have given you the **Three Spheres, Four Major Components** , and

Four Basic Actions as essential insights to help you understand yourself, your spouse and marriage itself. You have a great opportunity before you.

If you are willing to try, the ABCs will help you gain more understanding about how you and your spouse can begin to have a more enjoyable marriage.

So now what are you going to do with the information you have received? Hopefully you will choose to build and nurture your marriage.

The Hard Way

Most of what I will be sharing with you I have learned the hard way. It is my hope that this material will help you learn it in an easier fashion.

Take a look at the different letters. Pick one that looks interesting, or that might help you the most. Find the page and begin reading. May you have good success.

Practice

Remember what practice is? It is doing something over and over until it is normal behavior. When you begin to try one of the ABCs, don't just do it one time. Do it over and over.

Once again, you can be the hero – both to those around you and in your own heart.

It's Time To Start

The ABCs in Part II can be building blocks bringing you and your spouse the pleasure, sense of well-being and satisfaction you've longed for. They will help you troubleshoot your marriage. Each letter stands alone, independently. However when they are used together, their strength is increased. They are inter-related.

Just as life is intertwined, the ABCs are also intertwined in the **Three Spheres**, the **Four Major Components**, and **Four Basic Actions**. They are user-friendly.

Do your marriage problems seem as enormous as Mt. Everest? Do you know how to climb a mountain? One step at a time. So let's start climbing.

Let's Begin!

PART II – EQUIP

The ABCs of Marriage

APPRECIATE YOUR SPOUSE

Appreciation is one of the main building blocks that will help nurture your marriage. It is wonderful to have someone appreciate you, to be thankful you are alive. Usually it is easier to appreciate the similarities you have together rather than the differences. You're glad both of you enjoy the same kind of entertainment, the same food, the same friends. It's interesting that the axiom "opposites attract" often becomes a source of pain and difficulty as your relationship matures. The differences that you used to love with your spouse soon begin to frustrate you.

Often a specific difference that we have with them can be very frustrating. For example, they love to go to bed early in the evening and get up later in the morning than you. Their idea of being somewhere on time means before the event is over. When they bring order to something, you are confident only they could find where they put it. Their idea of intimacy is quite different than yours. They even want you to share what you are really thinking.

All of these situations are opportunities for you to either build up or tear down your marriage. Each opportunity gives you the chance to respect your spouse or to create tension. Each area of difference creates the opportunity to be annoyed or find a way to appreciate the difference.

Different in Communication

One of the most obvious ways that we are different from our spouse is the way we communicate. I will say more about this later, but for now, consider when the husband walks in the door from a trip and his wife asks him how his trip was. Many husbands will quickly respond, "Fine," and consider the question answered. His wife, however, wants far more. When she comes home from a trip and he asks her how her trip was, it may often take an hour or more for her to share all the events that took place on her trip.

She is longing for connection, for intimacy. Conversation is one of the main ways it is achieved. This need is usually greater in a wife than a husband. This is a very important difference. One can either be appreciative or aggravated by it.

Gratitude

Being grateful that you are married to your spouse will illustrate for them appreciation. It is wonderful to have someone thankful for you. To know that you are loved. To know that they want to be with you.

When you got married, you said you wanted to be with your partner for the rest of your life. If you are the groom, when your bride walked down the aisle, hopefully you were happy to see her. You were captured with her beauty and couldn't wait to make love to her and spend the rest of your days together.

If you are the bride, when you saw your groom waiting for you, hopefully your thought was, "I am such a fortunate person to be getting married to this man. I can't wait to be with him all the time."

I hope that those feelings are still true for you and your spouse today. If they aren't true, this book may be a key to helping you adjust your current view.

Jumping for Joy

I heard the story told of a man who was being mentored by another. Each time the mentor would see him, the mentor would jump up and down for joy because he was so happy to be with his student and friend. Imagine being on the receiving end of that kind of behavior.

I have experienced this feeling with my grandchildren. When they come over to our home, it is so wonderful to be with them. They know I love them. They look forward to coming to Grandpa's house. They are so excited to see me because they know I appreciate them.

To have someone appreciate you is a wonderful feeling. When was the last time you felt like jumping up and down for joy when you saw your spouse?

Evaluate: Why You Appreciate Your Spouse

1) What are some of the reasons that you appreciate your spouse?

a. _____

_____

b. _____

_____

c. _____

_____

2) Ask your spouse why they appreciate you. Write their comments down.

a. _____

_____

b. _____

_____

c. _____

_____

There will be many opportunities throughout this book to write down your reflections. Sometimes you will want to share these with your spouse. Other times they are simply to help you evaluate what is really going on and help you improve your relationship. Remember, this book is about the three E's: **Evaluate, Equip and Encourage.**

We Need To Be Appreciated

Many times when couples come and see me, though they don't realize it, they are simply looking for someone to appreciate them. This is true for both wives and husbands who want their spouse to be thankful for all they do in the home and for their hard work providing for the family. They often feel that they are taken for granted. One of the most common requests I hear is that one's spouse would greet them with appreciation rather than complaints.

If you are one of those who does not appreciate what your spouse does for you and for your family, or if you assume that is their job anyway, you are not nurturing them in a way that is going to encourage them and draw them closer to you. This way of thinking hurts you both. Being appreciated helps fill the giver and the receiver's life with joy.

They Just Don't Listen

Some people tell me that they are constantly giving encouragement and thanking their spouses, but it doesn't do any good because their mate still doesn't feel appreciated. One of the issues that we are going to look at is how to make sure they are able to hear your encouraging words in letter L. I also have tips to help you hear what your spouse is saying.

It's Often Miscommunication

Many problems in marriage are a result of miscommunication. It is possible that solving this dilemma may require more than reading this book and applying the principles. However, expressing appreciation and making sure you're heard is a great first step in creating a healthier marriage.

Take this opportunity to tell your spouse how much you appreciate them. Describe to them what it is that you appreciate about them.

The first building block of nurturing your marriage is appreciation.

A – Appreciate Your Spouse!

BELIEVE THE BEST

There is a description in the Bible, in the book of I Corinthians 13:4-8, that describes what love in a marriage is supposed to look like. It says:

- Love is patient and kind. Love is not jealous or boastful or proud or rude.
- Love does not demand its own way. Love is not irritable, and it keeps no record of when it has been wronged.
- It is never glad about injustice but rejoices whenever the truth wins out.
- Love never gives up, never loses faith, is always hopeful, and endures through every circumstance.
- Love will last forever.

— Holy Bible, New Living Translation,
copyright © 1996 by Tyndale Charitable Trust

This is one of the most quoted verses from the Bible. One of the pieces of wisdom that can be gained from this verse is if you can believe the best about your spouse in all situations it will benefit your home. This means giving them the benefit of the doubt even at times when it appears unbelievable. This is another basic building block for a more fulfilling marriage.

Appropriate Boundaries

Of course, there are appropriate boundaries when we talk about believing our spouses. I am not encouraging you to continue any codependent or enabling behavior that helps your spouse avoid living responsibly. If you have been constantly lied to or promised things that never happen, it will be extremely difficult to begin to practice this principle. We will talk about what is a healthy boundary regarding believing the best in the next few pages.

It's Hard

It is hard to believe the best about your spouse when they have continued to fail you by not keeping their word and have continued to take advantage of your good will. They've told you they would be home at a certain time and yet that time comes and goes and they still are not home. They don't call to let you know they will be late and apologize. They just show up late expecting you to understand. Why would you believe them this time? If you are constantly being lied to, it is difficult to trust.

They're Ready – You're Not!

It is not uncommon for a couple to show up at my office for help and one spouse is finally ready to get it right, but the other has given up. They wonder how come it took so many years for them to want to get help. They have been hurt so many times that they can't stand to be hurt again.

If your spouse is sincerely ready to make it work, then one of the most important things you can do is to begin to try to "trust them." I am talking about when your partner realizes that now is the time for change. This does not mean that you place yourself in a position to be taken advantage of or abused; it simply means that you try to begin giving them a chance again.

A Place of Accountability

One of the reasons that people come to see me is so that I can be a place of accountability for their spouse. For example; Jason and Heather sit down with me. Heather has been trying to get Jason to change his behavior for over 10 years. Her two children are now old enough that their father's disrespect, dishonor, lack of a good work ethic, and a different moral system than her own has finally led her to call it quits.

They have tried counseling once or twice before with very little help. She tells him to leave. He leaves for a few days, expecting Heather to call and ask him to come back because life without him will be too hard.

What Jason doesn't know is that for the first time in years, she is experiencing peace in her home. The children miss dad; however, even they are doing better.

He Calls for Help

By the end of the second week, Jason calls me. I meet with him and he tells me his story. I encourage him to ask Heather to come and meet with me. She comes with him and hears him express a desire to change, something she has heard before. She wonders if he is playing some kind of game with her to get her back. Is he going to be a really nice guy for the next few weeks and then when he is back in the home and things are going well, turn into the old guy again?

She wonders if he is really sincere. Does he truly want to change? Is he open to being confronted and instructed regarding his behavior in order that he might change? She needs to see some proof.

It helps her to have someone like me who has heard her story so that if he goes back to being the old guy, she has support from someone who can understand why she is quitting.

Jason is also hesitant to try again because he usually feels like a failure around Heather. He just never seems to get it right. I hope to be able to help him understand what his wife wants and find success instead of failing all the time.

When Someone Believes in You

Many times I have watched a husband or wife be challenged by their spouse to change and actually change. They begin to understand them, love them, and make changes that will benefit their marriage. Their positive response is often connected to someone believing the best about them. This is part of my function as a life consultant, to let them experience being trusted. It is much easier for me to believe that they are sincere in wanting to change since I haven't been the one who has been lied to and hurt many times before.

I try to establish enough of a trust foundation with the offended spouse in order that they can actually begin to believe their spouse. This ABC principle is challenging to embrace, but has great power to repair and restore a marriage.

The Power of Being "Believed In"

It is easy to see the power of someone believing in another. Watching children get encouraged by their coach or parent is almost like seeing them receive extra power or energy. Hearing the phrase, "You can do it!" brings a spouse hope that they can succeed in their marriage and actually empowers them.

You Must Look at the Past

If you have tried to make your marriage work, you have probably given your spouse many chances to respond differently. The wounds you have suffered, the hurts and disappointments that have been a part of your life for the past years have to be identified and reconciled if you are ever going to be able to "believe the best" again.

You are going to need to see some results, like her/him actually keeping their word and following through on things, in order that you can begin to believe them.

If you are to become healthy in your marriage, it is important to identify the places where you have been hurt emotionally — the places where you have been let down or disappointed in the past.

Think about those places of hurt or pain that were caused by your spouse. It might be necessary for you to also address things that happened before you got married. Often the wounds that our spouses inflict are similar to our experiences from when we were growing up. Both offenses caused before you were married and during your marriage need to be identified and processed in order that your marriage can be strengthened. Understanding why you are hurt or how you have hurt your spouse will help you begin the journey to be able to believe the best about them.

Evaluate: Places You Have Been Hurt

Take time to identify any places of hurt and offense from your spouse that are still in your mind which cause pain. For example: being lied to, disappointed, hurt in a specific way, etc.

1. _____

   _____

2. _____

   _____

3. _____

   _____

If you have not talked about these with your spouse, it is time to get some help. Go to them first if you feel like it is a safe place. If that doesn't work, call a friend, your spiritual leader, a counselor, or someone you trust who can help you begin to work through these issues.

If you are going to be able to trust your spouse again, it will be important that they recognize these places of pain. Hopefully, they will understand why you are bothered by these situations, tell you they are sorry and ask you to forgive them and give them another chance.

Doing the Basics

If you are the one who has hurt and offended your spouse by your behaviors and you want them to trust you again, you must recognize where you have hurt them, tell them you are sorry and make a sincere effort to change. They may or may not be able to forgive you. If they do forgive you, they may not be able to forget what happened. Forgetting often takes a long time. Hopefully they won't keep bringing it up all the time to remind you how you have hurt them.

You can begin to bring healing even if you miss the mark by not being defensive and remaining teachable when you are confronted in areas of your life that need to change.

Evaluate: Places You Have Hurt Your Spouse

Take time right now to identify the places where you have hurt or offended your spouse. If you can't think of any, go and ask them to help you identify one or two.

1. _____

_____

2. _____

_____

3. _____

_____

After you have identified these issues, you need to talk to your spouse about them. Ask them to forgive you in order that closure can be brought to these events. It is difficult to move forward when there are old hurts and wounds that are still painful. You may need to get some help either from a friend or a counselor to process these things with your spouse.

It Will Help

If your spouse is sincere and really does want to change, it will help your marriage if you try to believe the best. It may be helpful to find someone in your life that is able to hold you and your spouse accountable for the things that you say you will do. As a life consultant that is another part of what I do with the people who come and see me.

Helpful in Other Relationships

This principle of "believing the best" is also profitable in your other relationships. It can be especially helpful in raising your children. Children long to have someone believe in them. We will speak more about this under letter P – Parenting.

Believing the best is a difficult assignment, but a principle that will greatly enhance your marriage.

B – Believe the Best!

CONFESS WHEN YOU ARE WRONG

There is such power in saying the words, "I'm sorry," that it is amazing it is not said more often to help a marriage succeed. Years ago there was a line in a movie that said, "Love means never having to say you're sorry." That is simply not true! Love is all about saying you are sorry.

Why is it so hard to say, "I'm sorry"? One reason is that when you say it, it means that you are taking responsibility for your actions. Unfortunately, taking responsibility for one's actions is not something that has been fostered in great measure these past few years. In fact, just the opposite is often proclaimed as the new message of the day.

That message of the day sounds like: "It is somebody else's fault that I acted the way I did." When we confess that we made a mistake, we are admitting that we didn't get it right. The person we are confessing to is expected to believe that we are sincerely sorry and that we will try to change our ways. Because nobody is perfect, the need to say I'm sorry will always be present.

Saying You're Sorry

When you say you are sorry, it might mean that restitution needs to be made. You may need to replace something that you have damaged. You may need to make something right and probably need to change your behavior. This is also part of confession.

Admitting that you are wrong, that you made a mistake, has often been interpreted as being weak. It is actually an act of strength. Just saying you are sorry is often not enough. It takes courage to be able to clearly identify what you did wrong and indicate a desire to change. This will give your spouse hope that you want to change and that you will act differently.

What Do I Confess?

I am often asked, "What do I need to confess and how much do I need to tell?" If you are involved in alcoholism, drugs, gambling, theft, lying, cheating, tax fraud, or any other major area, you need to begin to tell your spouse in order that these areas in your life can be confronted, and that you can get help to stop these behaviors.

If your spouse is the guilty party, look for an opening to speak to them about what they are doing. If they don't or won't hear you, you need to get help for them in order that they can stop the destruction happening by their actions. I am only going to address two specific areas, adultery and pornography. Both take an unbelievable toll on marriages. Both need to be confessed.

Confessing Adultery

In a marriage when one person has committed adultery, there are some who would say, "You've already hurt your spouse once, so don't hurt them by telling them about your act of unfaithfulness." In my opinion, keeping your infidelity a secret is not the best way to achieve a marriage that will last a lifetime. Confessing your act of indiscretion will hurt them; however, keeping the incident a secret will, in the long run, hurt them far worse.

Confessing Looking at Pornography

When we talk about areas that offend our spouses, pornography has become a very explosive topic. Every week or so I see someone in my office who is having a problem saying no to looking at pornographic material either on the web, in videos or in print. Often those who are involved feel like it is no big deal. I disagree. Pornography most often is a danger for men. However, women are now also being caught by it.

It's interesting that many men, who might even struggle with keeping away from pornography, often are amazed that a woman could also be captured by its snare.

Most women in my office whose husbands have been found looking at pornography are greatly offended. Sometimes they say, "It would have been better if they had an actual affair." You might wonder, why? It's because it is harder to compete with a perfect, airbrushed picture that is just fantasy and not real.

Others have written plenty about the dangers of pornography. My point in even mentioning it in this chapter is that sometimes people feel it is something they can keep secret. If pornography is something you are engaged in looking at, confess it to your spouse and get help to break the addiction. Looking at pornography will rob you of intimacy with your spouse.

Asking Questions

I often tell the person who has been unfaithful that their spouse needs to be able to ask any questions about the incident without fear of being lied to again or meeting a resistant, defensive attitude. Not being defensive will help bring wholeness into your marriage.

How Much Do You Tell?

Your spouse may want to know the intimate details, or they may choose not to. If you tell them all the details, make sure that they understand that you don't want their minds focusing on the images you describe, especially when you are making love with them. More often than not, it is better if a more general description is given.

However, some spouses will not be satisfied with this. They feel if they are going to trust again in the relationship they need to know exactly what happened. It is a tough call, and a simple answer cannot be given. Each situation is unique. Choose as your main principle to honor your spouse and to repair the damage that has been done by your indiscretion.

How Many Times Can They Ask the Same Question?

Another difficult area concerns how many times do you need to answer the same question. For the first few weeks, answer as many times as they ask. You might say to them, "I've already answered that question before; what more do you need from me?" They might not need any more new data but just need to know that you are sorry, that you love them and that you are not going to leave them. Your marriage can survive adultery or pornography. It doesn't have to end in divorce. It is possible to have a stronger marriage if you and your spouse don't quit.

How Long Do the Questions Continue?

There will come a time when asking questions is no longer beneficial but rather detrimental. Again, there is no definite answer to this question. However, the need to ask questions could easily go on for several months. If it does go on this long, if you are the one being questioned, have patience. If you are the questioner, be sensitive to what the questions do to your spouse each time you ask them. Often the offending spouse just wants the event to be over, and actually revisiting it daily over a prolonged period will eventually do more damage than good.

I wish I could give you a more set answer, but I hope that these guidelines will help you restore your marriage.

No Secrets

Imagine living a life of no secrets with your spouse — a place where you don't have to hide anything. Living this way will help you build a marriage that will last a lifetime.

So What's Next?

Having shared with your spouse what you have done, and having asked for forgiveness, it will probably be time to find someone to help you process the pain and the fallout. Call your spiritual leader, your counselor, or a good friend so that they can help you figure out what to do next.

It Is a Lifestyle

When you begin the lifestyle of saying that you are sorry and admitting when you have done something wrong, it will help build trust in your spouse. It is important that your confession is sincere and that it is not just an attempt to get out of trouble with no thought of changing your behavior.

Evaluate: Places Where You Need To Confess

Take some time to identify places where you need to confess something that you have done wrong and may have hurt your spouse.

1. _____

_____

_____

2. _____

_____

_____

3. _____

_____

_____

After you have written these down, go and tell them you are sorry. Tell them of your desire to make things right. Tell them of the changes in your behavior you are willing to make.

Evaluate: Places Where You Have Been Hurt

Take some time to identify places where your spouse has hurt you.

1. _____

_____

_____

2. _____

_____

_____

3. _____

_____

_____

Now it's time to share these with your spouse. If you identify places where you have been hurt for several years, you probably don't want to tell them everything at one time. You rather need to tell them over time so that they can more easily process what has happened. This will help to bring more openness and honesty in your relationship.

Often one partner does not even know that they have hurt the other one. This is another reason that confession needs to become an important part of a marriage that will last a lifetime.

Evaluate: Places Where You Have Hurt Your Spouse

Ask your partner where they have been hurt by you and write their comments down.

1. _____

_____

_____

2. _____

_____

_____

3. _____

_____

_____

If you are able, tell them you are sorry, and that you desire to make things right. Also, tell them the changes you are willing to make in your behavior. Then begin to watch the healing process begin. It will take a while for them to forgive you and to be able to let go of the hurt and pain. It takes time to heal.

It's a Process

Finally, they may not believe you right away and may need to see some behaviors that indicate that you are sorry. That is just part of the process, so don't be discouraged. Just because they forgive you does not necessarily mean that they will trust you. Trusting you again will take time. Your words and actions will help prove that you mean what you said. When you are able to say you are sorry, it is a huge step in strengthening your relationship. Confession is often the beginning step to restoration.

C – Confess When You Are Wrong!

DATE ONE ANOTHER CONTINUALLY

Many of the ABCs require you to do something. Dating asks you to take time to be with your spouse. If you haven't been going on a date regularly, it is time to begin. If you have been going on dates consistently, don't quit.

When you first met your spouse, you probably went on dates. You picked them up at their home, or met them somewhere. You went to a movie, had dinner, and spent three-five hours or more alone enjoying each other's company. When people get married, the dating often stops. We will look at the reasons a little later.

Dating Makes a Statement

Dating communicates to your spouse that they are important, that you want to spend time with them. This includes a variety of things:

- going out for a meal
- shopping
- going to a show
- sitting at home watching a video
- listening to music
- eating popcorn together
- having a cup of coffee or a cappuccino
- going to a sporting event or some other type of event
- doing an activity together like, walking, bowling, fishing, golfing, etc.

The type of date you go on will depend on how much money or time you have. Whatever you decide, taking time to be with your spouse, and taking time to plan the event are statements that let them know they are important to you and that you love them.

Why Does Dating Stop?

I have wondered why it is that after marriage, for many people, going on a date with their spouse begins to happen less frequently. Here are several reasons that affect the frequency of going on a date.

- I have already caught my spouse, so what's the reason for going on a date?
- There are too many distractions in our lives.
- Money is too tight.
- Our interests have changed.
- I am not really feeling connected to my spouse, so why would I want to go hang out with them for several hours?
- What would we talk about?
- When we get together, we often hurt one another.
- Who's going to watch the kids?

Pursuit Doesn't Stop

If you feel like you have already caught your spouse, like the chase is over and you can quit pursuing them, you have made a grave mistake. Most people want to be pursued and romanced throughout their marriage.

Sometimes it's hard to pursue your spouse. Your life is too busy, it's hard to find a babysitter, work is too exhausting, and who has the energy to go on a date? When you get some free time, you just want to rest.

A Time of Relaxation

Going on a date should be a time of renewing your energy, a time of refreshment rather than a burden. It is important that the date not become a time when you talk about all your problems and the things that need to be done around the house. It needs to be a time when the problems going on within the family are not the main focus. The date time should not be a place where financial worries are discussed. These are important things to talk about in your marriage; however, make another appointment to talk about these issues. The date night needs to be a place of encouragement rather than one that leads you to feel depressed.

A Time for Enjoyment

The date time is for asking each other how they are doing. It is a time to look in each other's eyes and stare awhile in quietness. It is a time to enjoy being in the presence of the one you love and the one who loves you. It is a time to hold hands and tell each other how much you appreciate and love them. It is a time for laughing and enjoying one another's company. It is a time when you turn off your cell phone and pager and completely focus on each other. It is a time for your attention to be given to your spouse.

What Do We Talk About?

Sometimes couples tell me when they go out on a date they don't have anything to talk about. Here are several suggestions that might help you if this is your excuse. Talk about your:

- Hopes and dreams
- Current events
- Reflections on a book you have read, or a movie you have seen
- Tell stories from your past that will help your partner continue to understand you more.

Who Makes the Arrangements?

Either you or your spouse can initiate going on a date. If you don't know what your spouse would like to do, you can ask them. It is okay to work together as a team to schedule and plan your date. One person may be better suited to handle the logistics, while another is more able to handle the schedule. It is important that both spouses are dating each other.

Be Sensitive

When you go on a date, don't forget that appearance and smells are very important. Don't hesitate to get yourself cleaned up and put on some perfume or cologne. Husbands, opening a car door, helping your wife on and off with her coat or sweater, and dropping them off at the door are just standard operating procedures.

I remember one woman who met with me loved the acts of kindness that her husband did for her on their dates. He would bring small gifts, and would always open the car door. Don't forget your manners. Be thoughtful.

Evaluate: What You Can Do on a Date

List the things you would like to do on a date.

a. _____

b. _____

c. _____

d. _____

List the things your spouse would like to do on a date. If you don't know, take the time to ask them and write it down.

a. _____

b. _____

c. _____

d. _____

Kids and No Money

For those of you with young children and low funds, find other families who have children that you are friends with and trade nights watching each other's children once a week or every two weeks. This will help save money that you would have spent on babysitters. Make sure the people you trade nights with are kind and love your children. Make the night you have with the children a special time for them.

Making Your Spouse a Priority

Setting time apart to be alone weekly is a way to make each other a priority in your life. Planned dates and spontaneous dates are both important and valid. The date time should be written in your planner or on your calendar just like any other appointment. Nothing should take your date night's place except an emergency or death. It's too easy to lose it and lose contact with each other.

The date night also helps you keep common interests in your relationship through the years, not just being dependent upon children's activities, your job or your friends. Taking time to date your spouse is a great investment you can make in your marriage relationship. It is the commitment of time which says they are important.

The Result of Not Dating
- A disconnection with your spouse
- You don't know them as well
- A lack of intimacy
- Very little in common after 15-25 years
- During a mid-life crisis you don't know each other and it is difficult to support them.

Don't Wait To Begin Dating
With all these ideas, scheduling a date with your spouse should be a lot easier. Don't hesitate. Dating is a sure-fire way to help nurture your marriage. Make it happen soon! Plan it now.

When are you going on your date with your spouse?

Date: _____   Time: _____

What are you going to do?

_____

_____.

D – Date One Another Continually!

ENCOURAGE ONE ANOTHER

To encourage someone means to inspire with courage, to spur someone on. It is a kind note of appreciation and compliments for someone special. It is a word that enables a person to complete a task that seemed impossible.

There are many examples of how encouragement makes a significant difference in another's life:

- A child who is told they did a good job when they hit the ball, or when they struck out and were told that they would get another chance.
- The mom who feels stressed and worn out after cleaning, cooking and taking care of kids, and her husband thanks her for her hard work.
- The husband who has worked hard all day at the office and comes home to find his family grateful and appreciative for the sacrifices he makes.
- The wife who works outside the home and also takes care of her husband and home and knows her family is grateful.
- The husband who helps with the responsibilities of taking care of the house plus working hard to help care for his family, and his wife appreciates his efforts.

Many of us could increase the amount of encouragement we give to our spouses.

Who Has Encouraged You?

Think for a moment about the people in your life who have encouraged you. It might be a teacher, a coach, a parent, a relative, or a friend. Write down one or two of those who have encouraged you, and try to remember an example of just how they encouraged you.

Who encouraged you?

_____

What did they say or what did they do?

_____

_____

If you were not able to find anybody or list any stories, it is probably hard for you to be an encourager.

Evaluate: Places of Encouragement

Consider those places where you have encouraged your spouse. Make a list of them.

a. _____

b. _____

c. _____

d. _____

e. _____

If you haven't been encouraging your spouse, consider those places where you could encourage your spouse. Make a list and begin to share them with your spouse soon.

a. _____

b. _____

c. _____

d. _____

e. _____

More Tools To Help You

Here is a list that will help strengthen your relationship. It is a list of ways that will help you encourage your spouse. Several of these are applicable in other chapters. I have put them together to give you tools that can bring encouragement to your marriage.

1. Keep the wall of unresolved anger, hurt, and resentment from growing between you. *This encourages healthy communication.*

2. Do not keep a record of wrongs committed. *This encourages love.*

3. Provide equal opportunities for each person to discover and develop her/his unused strengths. *This encourages respect.*

4. Set aside regular time to communicate about what really matters to each of you. *This encourages intimacy.*

5. Recognize and affirm the strengths in each other. *This encourages honor.*

6. Make a scheduled date together. *This encourages connection.*

7. Develop your support group individually and as a couple. *This encourages honesty.*

8. Find a shared cause bigger than your relationship. *This encourages purpose and destiny.*

Encouragement is a life-giving addition as you nurture your marriage. Do it often.

E – Encourage One Another!

FAITH IS SIGNIFICANT

One of the areas that can be a place of peace and connection or a place of pain and disconnection is religion. Having a common spiritual experience is important as you strengthen your marriage. It is important to identify the areas of spirituality that have been your support and those that are getting in your way.

Conflict Begins

Let's consider Anthony and Sara. She has spent most of her 29 years worshipping in a congregation on Sunday mornings. When she met Anthony, she wanted him to go to church with her. He had never been raised in the church. A big part of his life was Sunday when he could rest, work around the house, go golfing and watch sports.

She has a relationship, not just with God, but also with the people of the congregation which she has been attending. You can see from this example that they have a dilemma concerning what is going to happen on Sunday morning.

When their first child, Tyler, is born, Sara wants to have him baptized. Anthony isn't particularly excited about this, but goes along with Sara to keep the peace. As Tyler gets older, Sara wants him to go to Sunday School with her. She has been going to church alone for the first few years of marriage anyway. She wants Anthony to join them as an example. He is not yet ready to give up his Sundays.

Conflict Increases

The ethical standards that Anthony chooses to live by, that are based in his own religious experience, have now become a point of contention. Sara is very frustrated. She doesn't know what to do. Maybe you find yourself in this same dilemma; your spouse does not want to participate in your religious experience. If both spouses are in agreement regarding religion, it will help make for a more peaceful, successful marriage.

A Little More of My Story

My wife and I both grew up in the Lutheran Church. We met in college, and both of us had a deepening spiritual experience where a relationship with Jesus Christ became a very meaningful part of our lives.

All of the principles that I am writing about in this book are taught and illustrated by Jesus. When my wife and I experience places of difficulty individually or together, we are able to find help from God for our situation.

The principles taught in the Bible have been the benchmark for the decisions we have made during our marriage. Having a common ground of belief has helped us during times and seasons of difficulty.

If you and your spouse are on different wavelengths regarding religion, it probably is a place of conflict or contention. It needs help.

Evaluate: What Needs To Change?

Describe what needs to change in your relationship with your spouse regarding the area of faith, your religious belief.

a. _____

_____

b. _____

_____

c. _____

_____

Take time to share what you have written with your spouse. This may be another place where you will need a counselor to help you sort through these issues.

So What Do You Do?

Let me share two basic points for the spouse who is frustrated with the religious beliefs, or lack of beliefs shared by their partner.

1. It is important that you not force them to participate in your religious faith.
2. Ask God to help change their heart so that they will be interested in sharing your religious experience.

If you are the spouse that is being forced to "get religion," here are two ways for you to handle the situation.

1. Let your spouse know that you are not interested in their religion.
2. Find some happy middle ground where you are comfortable and where you can participate in part of their spiritual activities.

It is important that you grant to your spouse the freedom to exercise their religious belief. If you beg them to change, whine about their lack of religious commitment, or shame them into worshipping with you, these options will all prove detrimental to your marriage.

It is always about honor, love, and respect. These three principles continue to be repeated time and time again as we look at the ABCs.

Your Opportunity

If you are reading this book and you have never had a relationship with God and with His Son Jesus, you can pray and ask God to be a part of your life. In my life I have found God to be a great source of help and encouragement. Having a life with God also means that I will be able to spend eternity with Him. I will live with the Lord forever.

If it is your desire to become a believer in God, you can simply recite this simple prayer:

Dear God, I want to know you. I want to believe in you and in your Son, Jesus Christ. Help me to believe. Forgive me for the things that I have done wrong and help me to live my life for you. Amen.

If you prayed this prayer, it is important for you to find a place of worship to exercise your newfound faith. Find a church and begin the joy of being a Christian. You can write a note to me at the address listed in this book, or at **gustafsonconsulting.org,** and tell me about your decision to become a follower of God.

F – Faith Is Significant!

GENTLENESS IS VERY VALUABLE

Expressing gentleness towards your spouse is another important part of nurturing your marriage. People who reflect gentleness to others will often be gentler with themselves.

A gentle person is described as someone who is self-controlled, slow to give or take offense, humble in spirit, lowly in mind and teachable. They have a mildness about them that is very attractive. They do not easily react negatively.

Gentleness: Masculine?

Gentleness is not usually associated with being masculine. However, I disagree. My experience has taught me that many women are looking for a man that will be gentle, tender, caring, and soft in his responses towards her. I am certain that many husbands want their wives to reflect gentleness.

Gentleness is not the same as passivity. Being passive is usually not an ingredient of a flourishing marriage.

The Angry Man

When Tracy and Mark got married, she was attracted to his mild-mannered personality. In fact, she used to call him Clark Kent, which was the identity that Superman used to disguise himself. As their marriage went along, Mark began to get more and more stressed. Their money was always tight. The pressures of raising their two children began to get on his nerves. Their house was usually a mess, and he felt like the children didn't respect Tracy or him. They both worked outside of the home, and several hours during the day their children were in daycare. It doesn't take a marriage expert to realize that their marriage was headed for trouble.

Mark began to grow increasingly irritable and one day yelled at Tracy for something that, as they discovered, was very insignificant. The frustrations had been building for a long time.

Through counseling, he discovered that his gentleness was really passivity. He had grown up in a home where voicing an opinion was not an option. He learned to be quiet. He took his frustrations and stuffed them, didn't deal with them, and eventually they all came out.

When Mark and Tracy finally showed up at my office, they were ready to divorce. The gentle man that Tracy had fallen in love with was no where to be found.

During the next several months, Mark was able to begin to share his frustrations, not just regarding his marriage, but even his experiences as a young boy growing up. He really was a gentle man and preferred peace. He needed to learn how to begin to speak what was really going on inside of him instead of burying it inside. He needed to become more aware of his emotions during the moment.

Tracy, who had never really had to listen to his opinion or ideas because he didn't share them, had to learn how to hear her husband. At times she was frustrated. Since Mark was now speaking, she was no longer always getting her way.

Marriage Is About Change

Marriage is a constant, changing experience. It begins in the ecstasy of attraction, meanders into self-discovery, which is often painful, and hopefully culminates in an intimate, joyful, lifelong union.

Whether or not you realize the full potential of this vision depends not on your ability to attract the perfect mate, but on your willingness to learn more and more about who you are and what is important to you and your spouse. As you are learning about yourself, your spouse and what it is like to be married, practicing gentleness is a great way to help nurture your relationship.

Gentleness Is Required

In a marriage, conflict will occur. When it does, gentleness is required. Here is a list of some very basic principles of fighting fair, or as I prefer to call it, healthy arguing.

Principles of Fighting Fair (Healthy Arguing)

- Share honestly from your heart
- You are not there to conquer
- Look for ways to find agreement
- Let your love and understanding draw you closer
- Ask yourself: Do I simply want to win? Or, do I want to enrich our relationship and grow together as a team?
- Only one person winning actually means both lose
- Both need to win
- Don't run from strife
- Avoidance is always trouble
- Don't sandbag – process as soon as possible
- Put aside your false expectations
- Identify your and your spouse's hot spots
- Know what is worth fighting about
- Grow in your understanding of yourself and your spouse
- Timing is everything
- Choose your battles carefully
- Major on the major issues, not on the minor issues.
- Some differences are just differences, not worth the fight
- Admit when it is your fault
- Speak the truth in love
- A gentle answer turns away wrath
- Choose a time to talk when you are not tired and when it is convenient for both of you.

You Both Win

You need to be constantly looking for the plan that will help you both win. I use the word winning here not in the sense of the other person being defeated. If the other person feels defeated, nobody really won. This type of winning does not encourage you to have to be the one on top. This type of winning involves actually being willing to give up your agendas. This type of winning is rooted in respect, honor and love.

Poison Traps

Don't fall into the following "poison traps":

- Give-up put-downs
- Don't dwell on downers
- Don't bring up past mistakes
- Avoid negative actions such as defensiveness, stonewalling, blaming, sarcasm, yelling, crying, and criticizing
- Avoid blaming

The Process of Conflict Resolution

When you break down the process of conflict resolution into small steps, this is what it looks like:

1. Know what you are fighting about. State the issue, give it clear definition and make sure you both agree.
2. Clarify the issues.
3. Know what you want out of the conversation. What is your end goal?
4. Take turns sharing your thoughts and feelings. Remember tone of voice.
5. Be aware of your own feelings. Be aware of your specific emotions, thoughts and feelings throughout the process.
6. Make it a two-way dialogue, not a monologue.
7. Give responses to one another.
8. Restate what you think the other person is saying in order to clarify. Listen carefully.
9. Ask questions if you do not understand something.
10. Stick to the subject/issue at hand.
11. Presume innocence.
12. Believe the best.
13. When you think you have talked it out, share what you think the conclusion is.

The Bottom Line

Find agreement. Don't let the sun go down without bringing some closure to the conflict. If no conclusion is reached, set a time to continue. In the meantime, try to understand your spouse's thinking and position.

All of the ABCs are a package deal. They work together. The synergy of doing several ABCs benefits you even more greatly than if you were just doing one of these principles.

Evaluate: How Have You and Your Spouse Been Gentle?

Make a list of the ways that you have been gentle with your spouse in the past month.

a. _____

_____

b. _____

_____

c. _____

_____

Now list two times that your spouse as been gentle with you in the past month.

a. _____

_____

b. _____

_____

Often They Just Don't Know What You Want

One of the first things that I always do with a couple when they come and visit me is to ask them what it is that they want and need in their marriage. After they have identified their needs and wants, I encourage them to share these with their spouse.

I have already made reference to this. It is worth mentioning again because it is a continual part of a strong marriage when each partner is sharing what they want and need. When it is possible or reasonable, have your spouse try to help you get what you want or need. This is a great way to continue to strengthen your marriage. As you share what you need and want, let gentleness be your constant companion.

Love Makes the World Go 'Round

We haven't talked a lot about love; however, it is obvious that love is the underwriting principle behind all of the ABCs. The love I am speaking of is a willingness to give up what you want, honor your spouse, and put them first.

If both partners pursue the principles of healthy arguing, their marriage will be more delightful. It is a wonderful thing to have your spouse looking for ways to serve you, honor you, and give to you. It is also a wonderful thing when you begin to look for ways to serve, honor, and give to your spouse.

Summary

- Be a united team
- Honor your spouse
- Purpose to have a winning situation
- Develop a plan where both partners win.

G – Gentleness Is Very Valuable!

HARDHEADEDNESS IS NOT AN ADVANTAGE

Just what is being hardheaded? It is not listening to your spouse. It is not being open to what they are saying. It is having your mind already set so that you won't even consider their opinion. It is being stubborn.

What is the opposite of being hardheaded? It is when you are teachable, willing to hear, and open to changing your opinion.

Wanting To Be Heard

In a marriage, one of the main things that a spouse wants to be certain of when they speak is that their partner will consider their opinion. Hardheadedness sets a person up for failure. If you are to strengthen and nurture your marriage, listening to one another and being open to each other is very important. If you or your spouse is hardheaded, it will impact every area of your life.

Expectations Can Mean Trouble

Expectations often are a real problem. They get in the way of what is really possible, and sometimes they help create resentment that is difficult to let go of. A very common expectation, and an appropriate one, is that our spouses will respect our opinions and listen to us. They won't be hardheaded. In listening to us, they might even consider our opinion and change their mind.

Hardheadedness Opens the Door to Divorce

It is common for people to marry thinking that it is okay to divorce. If you enter marriage with the idea that you can quit anytime, the odds of you having a marriage that will last a lifetime are significantly decreased. Let me share some thoughts about divorce. Here is how divorce begins:

1. First there is disillusionment
2. Then there is persistent tension
3. Then comes detachment.

First a person chooses someone to marry. They get married, move in and live together. Once they've had a chance to settle in, they get their first close look at the person they are living with. If they like what they see, they stay put. If they don't, they get frustrated, get out of the marriage and begin to look around for another person to marry.

There is a lot of pain in switching partners. The agony of dividing up children and possessions and putting aside treasured dreams leaves lasting scars. When one person goes through a divorce, they often become reluctant to risk intimacy again. They fear that the next relationship might also fail.

One of my hopes in writing this book is that I can help slow down the rate of divorce. Maybe I can even help reverse the trend by helping people not just survive in their marriage, but thrive. If your marriage is in trouble, it does not have to end in divorce. There is another way.

It is possible to identify those places that need help and to address them in order that your marriage can continue until, as the vow says, "Till Death Do Us Part." Don't lose hope. Begin to implement several of the ABCs and watch what happens. It is possible to have a marriage that will last a lifetime.

A Surprise

Usually one of the spouses is surprised that their other half is thinking about divorce. Divorce causes a great deal of pain for all the participants. There is emotional damage to the children and family members of the couple getting divorced. The children often grow up feeling responsible for the divorce and wonder if they will ever experience lasting love in their marriages. Some spouses think the only alternative to divorce is to stay in the relationship, just tough it out, and put up with a disappointing relationship for the rest of their lives.

Divorce doesn't just happen overnight. It happens over time. It is often the result of one partner being hardheaded. It only takes one person to want to get a divorce. If they have already given up on the marriage, without a miracle from God, which sometimes happens, the marriage will probably be over.

When you weld two metals together, the metals become fused. They are almost impossible to break apart. When they are broken, the break is very rough, and often both parts have severe damage. A divorce is like breaking a weld. It often leaves lasting damage.

Obvious Marriage Killers

Marriage problems are almost always because of two people. Here are some of the ways that get us in trouble in our marriages. These marriage killers are usually the result of one partner being hardheaded:

- One spouse finds their value in straightening out the other.
- One portrays an attitude of superiority. They always seem to have to get their way.
- One is unable to respect the other and isn't able to submit to their ideas or opinions.
- One is unable to the trust the other because of negative experiences they have had previous to marriage. They bring their mistrust into the marriage.
- One is afraid of allowing another to influence their opinion, so they find it easier to not listen. They think if they "give an inch," their spouse might "take a mile."

Your Words Are Very Important

Sometimes when people are hardheaded, they begin to get mean with their words. When my wife and I got married, we observed that some of our friends were often very sarcastic and cutting toward their spouses. They would often be putting down their partner without even knowing it. We decided that in our marriage putting one another down and using sarcasm against each other would not be part of our communication between each other. This is a wisdom principle that will help you and is an obvious marriage helper.

How Did I Get Into This Mess?

Reading this book may have brought you face to face with several of your weaknesses. In fact, you might even be wondering how you got into the mess you are in. Don't give up. There is hope. Applying these principles, one at a time, can help to heal your marriage and give you hope when you feel hopeless.

Don't be overwhelmed with how big the task looks. Remember, the way you eat an elephant is "one bite at a time." The way to climb a mountain is one step at a time. Find that principle or two that you can begin to work on and just start. Doing something is almost always better than doing nothing.

Evaluate: Areas of Hardheadedness

List some of the areas in the last six months where you have been "hardheaded" in a dialogue with your spouse.

a. _____

_____

b. _____

_____

c. _____

_____

Now list two areas in the last six months where your spouse has been "hardheaded" in a dialogue with you.

a. _____

_____

b. _____

_____

Look at these areas and determine if you could be open to their opinion regarding one of these issues. Using the wisdom principles from the previous chapter, if you can find a place of willingness to consider the other point of view, and maybe even change your point of view, go quickly and tell them you would like to reconsider the area that you were so adamant about. Being teachable and open to hearing them is an essential ingredient as you nurture your marriage. Lay your hardheadedness aside.

H – Hardheadedness Is Not an Advantage!

INTIMACY WITH YOUR SPOUSE IS VERY SPECIAL

Men and women today are asking for intimacy in their marriages. Many don't even know what this word means. What some think that intimacy is, is really a very unhealthy, unrealistic, codependency.

Many times I meet with a couple and the wife will be longing for intimacy. She wants her spouse to be her best friend. The husband does not have a clue what intimacy is. He often says in his mind, "How come she's not happy with what she's got?"

What Is Intimacy?

Here is a list that I hope will give you a better understanding of what intimacy is:

- It is when you are accepted for who you are
- It is when romance and affection are shared
- It is when you are appreciated for the things that you do
- It is being accepted when you have failed
- It is when your spouse is aware of your presence
- It is when your emotional needs are being met
- It is when you feel secure, knowing that you are loved.

Being Hurt Makes Intimacy More Difficult

Intimacy is more difficult to achieve when one person in the relationship has been betrayed or hurt. A wall is set up in their heart to protect them from being injured again. If you are going to achieve intimacy, you will need to be vulnerable. Often being vulnerable is associated with being weak. Because our acceptance of each other is based upon what we think of each other, we are unwilling to let another get to know us for fear that when they find out who we really are, they won't like us.

Intimacy Takes Work

Closeness just doesn't happen because we live under the same roof and have the same name. I have heard it said that "just because you park a Ford in a Toyota garage doesn't make it a Toyota." Intimacy doesn't just happen. It takes work.

Do you accept your spouse for who they are? Do you feel accepted by them for who you are? Being accepted is a basic ingredient for having a marriage that will last a lifetime. If you do not feel accepted by your spouse, it will be difficult to experience intimacy. We already talked about the importance of appreciation under Letter A. Feeling appreciated is another way that our spouse can experience intimacy with us.

Are you affectionate towards them? Do you express it? Do they express affection toward you? Affection helps create increased intimacy.

If you know that you are approved of without having to meet their expectations, then you are experiencing intimacy.

Paying Attention Is a Priority

It is important that we pay attention to our spouses. It is not uncommon for couples to meet with me and talk about how their spouse hardly even notices that they are around. Paying attention to them will help draw you closer to them.

Showing them you love them by comforting them, encouraging them, respecting them and supporting them will help them feel more intimate with you.

Security Is Important

Another way that intimacy is increased is when your spouse feels secure with you. This is often more meaningful for wives than for husbands. Security can be as simple as your spouse knowing where you are or whether the bills are going to be paid. Intimacy is a place where you and your partner are at peace and at rest with your relationship with each other.

Security is your spouse knowing that when you are on the computer you aren't in a chat room with another person giving your intimacy to another. Security is them knowing that you aren't viewing pornography which is extremely dangerous to a marriage.

Evaluate: What About Your Level of Intimacy?

In light of what you have just read, ask yourself this question. After you are finished share these responses with your spouse.

Do you feel intimate with your spouse? _____.

Describe several times when you felt close to your wife/husband? When have you experienced intimacy?

a. _____

_____

b. _____

_____

c. _____

_____

In light of what you have just read, ask yourself this question. Once again, also share this information with them.

Do you think your spouse feels intimate with you? _____.

Describe two times when you tried to be intimate with your spouse?

a. _____

_____

b. _____

_____

I

It's Tough To Hide in Marriage

Some of you are longing for intimacy in your life. Hiding is not what marriage is about. Marriage means being in the spotlight, being under the increasing scrutiny of another person. Marriage is about truth at all costs. It is living a life with no secrets. Both spouses having confidence that they could walk into any area of their partner's life and not be surprised with a secret that would damage their relationship.

Marriage Often Is Not Gentle

Marriage is one of the most intense ways for people to come to know one another. The process of getting to know one another is often not gentle. It is a disciplined and effective means for helping men and women humble themselves and surrender their own wills.

You are forever being asked to let things go. You are also asked to give up your ideas and attitudes where you are being demanding and selfish.

Evaluate: Ways To Increase Intimacy

Write down several ways that you could increase intimacy in your marriage. (If you can't think of any, go back to the list on the previous page and transfer several of them that seem appropriate for your marriage.)

a. _____

_____

b. _____

_____

c. _____

_____

Throughout this book there have been ideas to help you nurture your marriage. Some of them are more difficult to implement than others. The examples listed in this chapter can be put to work right away. Increasing intimacy is possible. If you use these ideas to help nurture your marriage, you will be pleasantly surprised how well they work.

Intimacy is created by spending time together, sharing your heart through your conversations, and touching one another. If you are doing these three things in a spirit of love, respect, and honor, intimacy will be created and increased.

I - Intimacy With Your Spouse Is Very Special!

I

JOKING AT YOUR PARTNER'S EXPENSE IS HARMFUL

Much of my day is spent watching how people relate to one another. I listen to their words and comments, and then I watch the response of their partner. It is not uncommon to hear one spouse make jokes about the way their partner spends money, does chores, cooks, spends their time, dresses, sleeps, drives, works, eats, etc.

You can probably find a joke made about anything that happens between couples. There are some areas that seem less offensive than others, but jokes usually hurt someone.

Some Jokes Obviously Are Not Appropriate

Of course, there are areas in our marriage that we know it isn't wise to joke about, such as making love, our partner's weight or appearance. However, I propose that if you are trying to build a marriage that will last a lifetime, all comments that aren't constructive or uplifting are detrimental and cause greater hurt than you can imagine. Sarcasm, jokes, and unhealthy humor are destructive to our relationships.

There is room for humor in a marriage; however, when it is degrading, it is not profitable. Speaking the truth to one another is important; however, to do it in the form of a joke or sarcasm is not wisdom. Take time and listen to the comments you and your spouse make toward one another. You might be surprised to find out what you are actually saying.

A Result of Low Self-esteem

Derogatory jokes directed towards our spouse are often said because the person making the comment has low self-esteem. They need to tear another down and feel like they are better than the other person. They often have been joked about by others as a child. Being made fun of is very destructive for adults. If you are doing this behavior, you must stop if you want a stronger marriage.

Evaluate: Phrases or Jokes That Are Detrimental

Take time to identify words, phrases, jokes or comments that you have said to your spouse that have been discouraging or degrading to them. Write them on the following lines.

a. _____

_____

b. _____

_____

c. _____

_____

Take time to identify words, phrases, jokes or comments that your spouse has said to you that have been discouraging or degrading to you. Write them on the following lines.

a. _____

_____

b. _____

_____

c. _____

_____

As with the previous exercises in this book, these are the things that will eventually need to be shared with your partner. You may need a counselor, friend, or spiritual leader to help you talk about them. It is very important that the time comes when they are made known, processed and changed.

It Is Time To Put an End to It

If you are the one that is often joked about, it is time for you to put an end to it. The arrow that was put in your heart by the comments of your spouse needs to be pulled out if you are to have a marriage that is whole. When they acknowledge what they have done wrong, say they are sorry, purpose to change, and then change, they can then begin to pull out the arrow from your heart.

Check with Your Spouse

If you are not certain whether your words are intimidating or destructive, go and ask your spouse. If they identify you as one who is cruel with your words, quickly go, confess, and make it right. Go and re-read chapter C on confession if you have forgotten how. Often the person that is being joked about is not laughing.

Speaking words of encouragement and speaking well toward one another will do a great deal towards nurturing and building up your marriage. Being careful that your jokes and your humor are respectful is very important.

J – Joking at Your Spouse's Expense Is Harmful!

KNOWING YOUR SPOUSE'S NEEDS IS VITAL

Knowing your spouse's needs is very important. There is a difference between wants and needs. People need oxygen to live; however, wanting to drive a Porsche is just a want. It is surprising how many people don't know the answer to the question, "What do you want and what do you need?" for themselves or for their spouse.

I remember a young woman in my office who burst into tears after I asked her this question. After a few moments of her sobbing, I asked her what were her tears for? She replied, "This is the first time anyone has ever asked me what I wanted." Her husband just stared at me, aware that he had some things to change in his relationship with her.

What Is Important to You?
This chapter will hopefully help you to begin to identify what is important to you and also help you better understand your spouse. Your need and your spouse's needs are often connected to the expectations that you brought into your marriage. There are expectations that have helped to strengthen your relationship, and weaken your relationship.

It is important to know what your expectations were when you got married. For many couples, what they have ended up with is far from what they thought they would get. This creates great turmoil. If we can understand ourselves and our spouse's needs more completely, we will be better able to nurture our spouse instead of hurting them.

As you begin to discuss your expectations, let's try to understand the things that are important to you and your spouse.

Evaluate: Priorities
Rank your first three priorities. The three most important people to

you, the three ways you spend your money, and the three ways you spend your time. When you are finished, do the exercise trying to guess what your spouse's answers would be. Notice the difference. Let them try this exercise. Share this information with them and then compare your answers with each other.

Three Most Important People

To me:

1. _____

2. _____

3. _____

To my spouse:

1. _____

2. _____

3. _____

Three Ways Time Is Spent

By me:

1. _____

2. _____

3. _____

By my spouse:

1. _____

2. _____

3. _____

Three Ways Money Is Spent

By me:

1. _____

2. _____

3. _____

By my spouse:

1. _____

2. _____

3. _____

The goal of this exercise is to help you understand what is important to you and your spouse. It will help you see more clearly how you are different from them. This newfound knowledge can help nurture your marriage. You can use it to discover how to increase your love for your partner. For example, being more aware of your partner's needs and wants can help you when you serve them or buy them gifts.

We Are Made Differently

Part of the strength of a marriage is that each of us has been made differently. When we don't understand our differences, it often becomes an area of conflict. Here is a list of differences that will help you have a greater understanding for your spouse.

Different Priorities

Women often have different need priorities than men. Women need to be secure, feel protected, be courted throughout the whole marriage, need intimacy, want to be led, not pushed and forced, but led. There is a difference between pushing and leading. I will say more about this under letter N.

Men want to be honored, respected, comforted, and just would like to have a happy wife. This doesn't mean that women don't want to be honored and respected. However, the priority is different for men than for women.

We Don't Get What We Want

What often happens in marriage is we hope our spouse will meet our needs. However, they don't know what they are because we don't tell them. Or they do know, but they ignore them. If our needs are not being met, we will have trouble in our marriage. The pattern for a marriage that will last a lifetime is both people investing in the marriage, not just trying to see what they can get, but helping to provide what is important to their spouse.

Once we have gotten a clearer understanding of what our needs are, we might come to find out that they are not as important as we thought, and consequently they won't have as much power over our emotions.

As you consider your needs, here are some ideas that might help you better understand yourself. For example, you might say your need is to feel like you are important. You might want to feel that you are honored or can be trusted. You might want to be able to be free to be who you really are.

For some of you, this will be an easy task; for others of you this may be difficult or even painful. In a marriage that is moving toward wholeness, these needs must eventually be shared. But for now, just identify them.

Evaluate: Your Needs

Take a few minutes to reflect on your own needs.

What I need in my marriage:

1. _____

2. _____

3. _____

Now take a moment and consider whether these needs are being met.

The next exercise will help you discover the primary way you enjoy being loved. You will find out how you make a connection with your spouse and what counts most to you and them.

Bank Deposits

Gary Chapman has described in his book, *Five Love Languages* (Chicago: Northfield Publishing, 1992, used by permission), the different ways we love and are loved in our marriages. His understanding is very helpful. He recognizes that not everyone is touched by the same kind of love.

He introduces the concept of a bank deposit helping us to gain a clearer understanding of what being loved means. He asks the question, "What gets you a bank deposit?"

A "bank deposit" is something that is said or done that creates gratefulness and thankfulness and puts a deposit in you or your spouse's love bank.

Recognizing and understanding how our spouse enjoys being loved makes it easier to build them up and touch their heart in the ways in which they will personally respond. Both spouses are enriched and satisfied. This is how we touch one another's soul.

Chapman describes people loving and being loved in five different ways: Speaking words of love, Spending time, Giving gifts, Serving, and Physically touching one another.

On the following pages I have listed each of these ways of loving. I have given you ten lines to fill in and several descriptions of each one of these love languages. Write down as many ways of being loved as you can. If you can't fill in all the spaces, that is okay. Part of this exercise is finding out which language is easier for you to identify how you enjoy being loved.

Words of Affirmation

One way that people feel loved is when they are encouraged with words. This includes verbal compliments, words of encouragement, words of appreciation, a gentle tone of voice, words of love, and requests instead of demands. These words can affirm the self-worth of your spouse, create intimacy, heal wounds, and bring out the full potential of your mate.

Examples: I love you, thanks for helping me file my papers (wash dishes…), you really look nice, I'm so proud of you, I appreciate it so much, you're a good mom/dad, etc.

Write down words or phrases that you love to hear:

1. _____

2. _____

3. _____

4. _____

5. _____

6. _____

7. _____

8. _____

9. _____

10. _____

Spending Time

Another way people feel loved is when their spouse spends time with them. Our attention is focused on each other (free from distractions) and enjoying the time being together, thoughtfully listening to one another and sharing ideas, feelings and what we are really thinking. This will also include doing activities together that both spouses enjoy. All this communicates that we truly enjoy spending time together.

Examples: evening together (often away from home), meet for lunch, walking, cuddling, ride in the car, bicycling, antique shopping.

Write down things that you love to do with your spouse:

1. _____

2. _____

3. _____

4. _____

5. _____

6. _____

7. _____

8. _____

9. _____

10. _____

Gift Giving

Another way that people feel loved is when gifts are given to them. Gifts are visible symbols of love. This includes items that are purchased or made. Gifts demonstrate that you care. They represent that you value the relationship. They also illustrate what is important to you.

Examples: flowers, jewelry, cards, money, food, little notes, clothing, something I know is very special to my spouse and will touch her/his heart.

Write down things you love to receive:

1. _____

2. _____

3. _____

4. _____

5. _____

6. _____

7. _____

8. _____

9. _____

10. _____

Being Served

Some people feel loved the most when their spouse does something for them — when their spouse serves them.

Examples: helping around the house, washing the car, fixing a leaky faucet, keeping up with the laundry, cooking a favorite meal, housecleaning, back rubs, doing a job that your spouse usually does.

Write down what I love for my spouse to do for me:

1. _____

2. _____

3. _____

4. _____

5. _____

6. _____

7. _____

8. _____

9. _____

10. _____

Being Touched

For some, the way that they feel loved the most is by being touched by their partner. This can include the slightest reaching for and touching of their spouse's hand, all the way to passionate lovemaking. Touch becomes an amazingly powerful form of communicating emotional love.

Examples: touching throughout the day, putting your arm around your spouse while walking or sitting together, holding hands, kissing, hugging and holding one another (especially in a time of stress, pain or crisis), lovemaking.

Write down how you enjoy being touched:

1. _____

2. _____

3. _____

4. _____

5. _____

6. _____

7. _____

8. _____

9. _____

10. _____

How did you score? (What is the number of items on each list)

_____ Words of Affirmation

_____ Quality Time

_____ Receiving Gifts

_____ Acts of Service

_____ Physical Touch

Which of the preceding had the longest list? Look back over it. This one was probably the easiest for you to make, the one where thoughts flowed. It is probably the primary way that you enjoy being loved. You may have more than one.

Time for Your Spouse To Do the Evaluation

Now it is important that your spouse do the same thing you have just done in order that they might learn how they want to be loved. Give them this exercise and ask them to complete it for you so that you can learn more about how to more fully love them. This will help you continue to learn more about how to nurture your marriage.

Words of Affirmation

One way that people feel loved is when they are encouraged with words. This includes verbal compliments, words of encouragement, words of appreciation, a gentle tone of voice, words of love, and requests instead of demands. These words can affirm the self-worth of your spouse, create intimacy, heal wounds, and bring out the full potential of your mate.

Examples: I love you, thanks for helping me file my papers (wash dishes…), you really look nice, I'm so proud of you, I appreciate it so much, you're a good mom/dad, etc.

Write down words or phrases that you love to hear:

1. _____

2. _____

3. _____

4. _____

5. _____

6. _____

7. _____

8. _____

9. _____

10. _____

Spending Time

Another way people feel loved is when their spouse spends time with them. Our attention is focused on each other (free from distractions) and enjoying the time being together, thoughtfully listening to one another and sharing ideas, feelings and what we are really thinking. This will also include when we are doing activities together that both spouses enjoy. All this communicates that we truly enjoy spending time together.

Examples: evening together (often away from home), meet for lunch, walking, cuddling, ride in the car, bicycling, antique shopping.

Write down things that you love to do with your spouse:

1. _____

2. _____

3. _____

4. _____

5. _____

6. _____

7. _____

8. _____

9. _____

10. _____

Gift Giving

Another way that people feel loved is when gifts are given to them. Gifts are visible symbols of love. This includes items that are purchased or made. Gifts demonstrate that you care. They represent that you value the relationship. They also illustrate what is important to you.

Examples: flowers, jewelry, cards, money, food, little notes, clothing, something I know is very special to my spouse and will touch her/his heart.

Write down things you love to receive:

1. _____

2. _____

3. _____

4. _____

5. _____

6. _____

7. _____

8. _____

9. _____

10. _____

Being Served

Some people feel loved the most when their spouse does something for them. When their spouse serves them.

Examples: helping around the house, washing the car, fixing a leaky faucet, keeping up with the laundry, cooking a favorite meal, housecleaning, back rubs, doing a job that your spouse usually does.

Write down what I love for my spouse to do for me:

1. _____

2. _____

3. _____

4. _____

5. _____

6. _____

7. _____

8. _____

9. _____

10. _____

Being Touched

For some, the way that they feel loved the most is by being touched by their spouse. This can include the slightest reaching for and touching of their spouse's hand to passionate lovemaking. Touch becomes an amazingly powerful form of communicating emotional love.

Examples: touching throughout the day, putting your arm around your spouse while walking or sitting together, holding hands, kissing, hugging and holding one another (especially in a time of stress, pain or crisis), lovemaking.

Write down how you enjoy being touched:

1. _____

2. _____

3. _____

4. _____

5. _____

6. _____

7. _____

8. _____

9. _____

10. _____

How did you score? (What is the number of items on each list?)

_____ Words of Affirmation

_____ Quality Time

_____ Receiving Gifts

_____ Acts of Service

_____ Physical Touch

Which of the above had the longest list? Look back over it. This one was probably the easiest for you to make, the one where thoughts flowed. It is probably the primary way that you enjoy being loved. You may have more than one.

Now take what you learned from this exercise and begin to love your partner in the way they want to be loved. Take your score and show it to your partner. Compare your results.

Like You Are in the Mud

Have you been stuck in your relationship? Perhaps you've said the following: "I have been trying and trying to please my spouse and it doesn't seem to have worked. What I've done hasn't gotten me a bank deposit." Figuring out how your spouse wants to be loved may be your answer.

Remember, a "bank deposit" is something meaningful that increases her/his value, brings you closer, and makes your marriage better.

Think this way, "I am going to take my spouse's list and work each week at doing at least five things (small or large) that are meaningful to her/him until it is my normal, natural way of living. My job is to give them what they want and need. In turn, I may be amazed and surprised by how much I receive."

Here's the payoff: Trade lists. Forget about your own. It will be like the farmer who plants his fields and tends the crops as he goes about his daily life. The crop keeps growing. Before he knows it, it's harvest time and he takes his profits to the bank.

K – Knowing Your Spouse's Needs Is Vital!

LISTEN VERY CAREFULLY

Learning skills and techniques that will help you communicate more effectively with your spouse is another important element in nurturing your marriage.

Years ago, a mother and father were dependent on each other to survive in a way that is different from today. Dad went and hunted for the food. Mom took care of the kids and prepared the food when dad came home. Food, sex, children, shelter, and security motivated them to work together because the fulfillment of these basic needs required specific roles and skills.

Today things have changed. Now, usually both work outside the home to provide for the basic needs of the family. When each person gets done with their day they are usually exhausted and need time to rest. Life often does not afford them that luxury.

Another thing that has changed is most wives don't just want their husbands to provide for them, they want to have a relationship with them. They want their husbands to talk with them. They want to partner with them, especially regarding taking care of the house and the children.

Listening and Talking Are Related

Often men say to me, "When we have a discussion, she just doesn't understand what I'm going through." And far too often women say to me, "He never listens." These are the complaints I hear when spouses are talking about their partners listening habits. They want to be listened to.

Relationship Involves Dialogue

Your relationship with your spouse involves dialogue. It is a two-way process in which each of you discuss things that are of concern or interest to you. When part of the dialogue is lost, that part of your relationship is also lost. If you are going to do any talking you must be listening. Trying to understand what they are saying shows that you care for them. Listening can sometimes be as important in producing healthy change as psychological or medical help.

Just the Wrapping Paper

When you communicate, you are expressing meaning that is often beyond the words that you are speaking. The meanings are transmitted in visual signals, the sounds you make, pauses, your tone of voice, what you look like, what you leave out, and even the way you breathe.

What your partner receives from you as you communicate is often based not just on the facts, but on what they perceive you are saying. The words that you are speaking are just the wrapping paper, not the gift. The gift is often inside the spoken word.

Being Understood Is Healing

If you are to develop fully in this life it is helpful if your spouse understands you. I have heard it said that, "being heard is so close to being loved that for the average person they are almost indistinguishable." To say something you value deeply to your spouse and to have them value it equally by listening to it carefully and appreciatively demonstrates love.

Saying What Is in Your Heart

It is important for you and your spouse to be able to speak the things that are in your heart. To be able to speak openly and vulnerably is unbelievably powerful. Being able to speak without fear of being shamed or receiving reproach empowers you to be true to who you are. This helps nurture your marriage.

Having to conceal things can make you sick, and yet being able to share your heart brings healing. The energy poured into concealment depletes your strength. If you find it necessary to conceal things, it often leads to loneliness, depression, feelings of falseness, fear of being found out, and creates a desire to hide. Where trust is present, sharing your heart helps you get healthy.

What Is Effective Communication?

Effective communication is when your spouse properly interprets the meaning of your words. Your words may never perfectly match their understanding. However, you are responsible to clarify your message and make sure the impact felt is what you meant.

Three Different Styles of Communication

There are basically three different styles of communication when people talk with each other.

1. Talking in a degrading manner, which involves blaming, scolding, judging, belittling, instructing, and supervising.

2. Talking overly apologetic, which involves being ingratiating, groveling, and appearing to yield all of the time.

3. Having an equal give and take between each other and mutually listen to one another.

Obviously #3 works best.

Evaluate: What's Your Style?

What is your style of communicating? #_____.

What is your spouse's style of communicating? #_____.

Several Communication Principles

Let's say you have something important to discuss with your spouse. These principles will help you communicate more effectively.

- Take time to ask them when would be a good time to talk with them. This shows you respect them.
- Tell them how long you think the conversation will take.
- If they need to take a break while you are talking, let them. Very few conversations are ever won through force.
- Don't give up if they don't want to talk. Overcome the tendency to give in and not communicate.
- Make sure the tone of your voice is consistent with your content. People respond first to your tone.

- When your verbal message conflicts with your nonverbal message people respond more to your nonverbal message.

- When you offer a compliment and a criticism together they usually hear only your criticism.

- When your comments are connected with the word, 'but' they usually will not recall what was said before the word "but."

Core Conditions of Effective Listening

Here is a list of skills that enhances effective listening. These skills take practice, practice, and more practice.

- Respect: Honor, exhibiting a willingness to hear

- Warmth: Being present, paying attention to their words

- Empathy: Trying to see as they see

- Genuineness: Being open, honest, and transparent about your own thoughts and feelings, not phony

- A readiness to suspend judgment or evaluation

- Patience to wait while the other expresses their thoughts and feelings

- A commitment to work towards dialogue that enriches both

- Immediate feedback: sharing how you feel in the immediate present.

Trigger Words

Another key for effective listening is when you know the words that trigger instant emotional responses within you or your spouse. Take time to explore the negative experiences of these words. Try to understand why they have the meaning that they do. For some it is swear words; for others it might be a term from their childhood. As you come to understand these words, you can begin to prepare yourself when you hear them.

Evaluate: Trigger Words

Make a list of trigger words for you.

_____, _____, _____, _____, _____.

Identify your spouse's trigger words.

_____, _____, _____, _____, _____.

Being Silent When You Need To Be

It is tough to say the right thing at the right moment, but even more difficult to be silent when you know your words will only hurt. Understanding 'trigger words' can help you avoid saying things that will bring harm to your relationship.

How Your Spouse Perceives You Is Important

If your spouse is afraid that you will be unfriendly, they will be sensitive to anything that can be perceived as distant, cold, critical or rejecting. If they expect you to be hostile, they will see any absence of response or any neutral or slightly negative response as proof of your critical or malicious intent.

If they anticipate your support, they may interpret your silence as acceptance, your interest as evidence of approval or the sounds you make as a signal that you agree with them. If you are not in support or in agreement, you must let them know and not let them assume that you are in agreement with what they are saying.

Communication Stoppers
- Downplaying feelings
- Using put down questions or statements
- Problem solving too quickly
- Giving pat answers without thinking
- Asking closed-ended questions
- Asking questions with a hidden agenda
- Not owning your statements
- Talking too much and not listening enough
- Not making clear what you are saying
- Shifting topics before they are closed
- Having "a know-it-all attitude"
- Using "you should statements"
- Speaking in a commanding, loud, threatening voice

- Being too busy thinking about your response
- Being defensive
- Being sarcastic
- Being hardheaded
- Being angry
- Assuming instead of finding out the facts
- Acting like you are either arrogant or inadequate
- Having too much information

Men and Women Respond Differently

Most men and women talk and respond differently. A man walks in the door and the wife asks, "How was your day?" The husband says, "Okay." That's it for him. The woman still has a great deal she needs, and he thinks he's said enough. He has not even begun to give her his heart or mind. Often he has been giving it away all day and is exhausted. Sometimes when he has shared his heart or mind in the past, it hasn't been received.

We Hear Differently

You hear your spouse through the filter of your personality. If you are to understand them you must hear the differences in their personality. You are unique and one of a kind. It might seem like you understand what they are saying, but you often end up missing their true meaning.

What Is Fire Gazing?

Years ago fire gazing used to be a male occupation. You see the cowboys surrounding the campfire at night. Pictures of the Aborigines doing the same thing are often seen on the Discovery Channel. It is almost always men and not women in these pictures.

Think what happens now with the TV. Men come home from a hard day at work and plop themselves in front of the TV and fall asleep. It allows men to redirect their focus, stop thinking, and just relax. Several writers who talk about the differences between men and women correctly identify a man's need for cave time. It is my opinion that both men and women need cave time.

Cave Time

Cave time is a time when you can go and relax. It is a time to withdraw and to be alone. When your partner goes into the cave to be alone:

- Understand their need to withdraw
- Let them solve their problems, unless they ask you
- Don't try to nurture them by asking about their feelings
- Don't sit next door to them and wait for them to come out
- Don't worry about them or feel sorry for them
- Do something that makes you happy.

So let's begin to practice a little of what we have learned in this chapter.

Evaluate: Communication

Identify and affirm the strengths in your relationship by completing the sentence, "I appreciate in my spouse _____." Write at least three different items.

1. _____

_____

2. _____

_____

3. _____

_____

Take the time to read them to your spouse. Let your spouse know that their assignment is to hear you and to receive your gift of appreciation. Ask them to tell you what they heard. Make certain that what you said and what they heard is the same thing.

Let's try another one. Identify the growing edge of your relationship by completing the sentence, "I need from you ..." at least two times. State your unmet or partially met needs/wants in terms of behavior you would like from the other.

1. _____

_____

2. _____

_____

Once again, take the time to read them to your spouse. Encourage them that their assignment is to hear what needs and wants you are trying to make known to them. Once again, ask them to tell you what they heard.

Have them do this same exercise. Then ask them what they wrote. Identify and affirm the strengths in your relationship by completing the sentence, "I appreciate in my spouse _____."

1. _____

_____

2. _____

_____

Let's try another one. Identify the growing edge of your relationship by completing the sentence, "I need from you..." at least two times. State your unmet or partially met needs/wants in terms of behavior you would like from the other. When they are finished, have them tell you and make sure you hear them.

1. _____

_____

2. _____

_____

A Review of the Basics

- Purpose in your heart to try to understand what your spouse is saying before you judge them.

- Try to listen closely and not assume what they are saying.

- Don't be afraid to change and to grow as you hear your spouse speak.

- Always exhibit honor and respect.

L — Listen Very Carefully!

MONEY NEEDS TO BE HANDLED WITH CARE

"Sure, we can afford it! It's only money." The Bible has great wisdom regarding money. Here are three quotes that will help you as you understand how to use money.

In Proverbs Chapter 22 verse 7, it says, "The rich rule over the poor, and the borrower becomes the lender's slave." Proverbs Chapter 22 verse 9 says, "He who is generous will be blessed, for he gives some of his food to the poor." I Timothy Chapter 6 verse 10 says, "For the love of money is a root of all sorts of evil."

The first Bible verse talks about the dangers of borrowing money. The next verse describes what happens to a person who is generous. And the final verse indicates that if you love money it has the potential to become a beginning point for all types of evil in your life.

For most of us, a great portion of our lives will be concerned with acquiring and managing our possessions. Money is a place in our lives that is often a place for great frustration. It is supposed to be something that gives us freedom instead of bondage.

Evaluate: Money, You and Your Spouse

Here are some questions that will give you an idea regarding what the relationship is between you, your spouse and your money.

Is it your money, your spouse's money, or both? _____

Who manages the money? _____

Do you have separate bank accounts? _____

Are you saving your money? _____

Are you a spender or a saver? _____

How many credit cards do you have? _____

Is it okay to go into debt? _____

Do you have a budget? _____

Do you have an emergency fund? _____

Is it okay to take a vacation? _____

How many times can you eat out a week? _____

Do you have insurance? _____

Who or what sets the standard for the use of your money?

_____

Do you and your spouse want to give a portion away? _____

Are you preparing for the future? _____

Whose Money Is It?

Let's look at each one of these questions. If you consider the money you and your spouse have as "your" money and not hers, I would venture to guess that your spouse may not feel like they partner with you in this area. If you feel like it is their money, ask yourself whether you really like this arrangement.

Knowing that all the money in your home is both yours and your spouse's creates an ownership for both of you that is healthy. You are aware as you spend or save your money that it is impacting both of you. You might have separate accounts with a portion of your funds that each one of you is responsible for. This gives you the opportunity to spend some funds without your spouse being involved, for example, birthdays, gifts, etc.

Who Manages Your Money?

Whether you or your spouse manages the money is not necessarily the issue. The important issue is that both of you are involved in knowing how much money you have and where it is going. For example, if the husband simply hands his check to his wife at the end of the pay period and then she gives him a certain amount for an allowance, this can be all right if he is also involved in knowing where the money is going and doesn't simply leave all of the responsibility to his wife.

Are You a Saver or Spender?

Usually in a family one is a saver and one is a spender. One is more comfortable with debt than the other. Whether you have debt or not, it is necessary that you have a savings plan.

Take a moment and write the answers to these questions.

How many credit cards do you have? _____

How many does your spouse have? _____

What is your total indebtedness, including your house? _____

Write down your answers. Then go and ask your spouse these questions and see what their answer is.

Most people do not know the answers to these three questions. They are very important questions. Knowing the answers to these questions can help you manage your money instead of it managing you.

Do You Have a Budget?

Budgets are necessary for almost every company that is in business. If they are so important for a business to succeed, why would you think they would be less important for your household to succeed financially? Budgets help you see how much money you have, where your money is supposed to be going and where it is going. At the end of this chapter I have included a very simple budget form that I use for all of my clients. Take some time and fill in the blanks.

If you are to build wealth, creating and maintaining a budget will help you begin the process of saving money and getting out of debt.

It is important to learn to live within your means, learn to spend less money than you make and start a savings and investment plan. If you follow this simple strategy, you will be well on your way to becoming debt free, living a more stress free life, and achieving wealth over time.

Where Do You Begin?

The first thing I encourage people to do when they come to me for help with their finances is to keep a record of every penny they spend in the next thirty days. This helps them identify where their money is going. Try this for yourself and see how you spend your money.

Worrying over investments, savings, or assets can cause increased stress. This can also happen if a couple purchases a major item on credit knowing that they are already behind in their average monthly obligations. Until a person has brought his or her debts under control, no real peace will ever be realized.

What About Specifics?

An emergency fund can save you the stress of putting your expenses on a credit card. I will address the issue of vacations under the letter *V*; however, financing them can be a part of the budget process. Whether you can eat out or not, and how many times, comes under the entertainment part of your budget.

There are different understandings about insurance. It is not my purpose in this book to talk about whether to have it or not. My intent in even mentioning it is to let it be a discussion point for you and your spouse as you begin to establish a budget.

Are you and your spouse on the same page regarding giving a portion of your finances away to charitable organizations? This also is a place of conflict for some couples. Who or what determines how much you give away if you do, and who your money goes to? These are important discussion questions as you consider how you and your spouse view money.

Finally, preparing for the future involves your investment plan, your savings accounts and how you hope to take care of yourself and your family as you grow older. These questions are not meant to depress you, but rather to help you address the financial concerns in your home.

The symptoms of financial stress are many. There are times when medical bills, unemployment, or a natural disaster occur in our lives that create financial despair and hardship. Oftentimes, however, our financial difficulties are often related to our own irresponsibility, immaturity, or lack of knowledge and wisdom. The area of money management often causes people to feel hopeless. Once again, you climb a mountain one step at a time. So, don't get overwhelmed; start with just a couple of principles in this chapter and see if it doesn't begin to help.

Money and Conflict

Money causes a great deal of conflict in marriages. You may need to address the way your spouse handles money. Because of the conflict that occurs when you do this, you may feel that it's not worth it. Let this book be a new beginning for you. Putting off speaking to them any longer will probably only increase the difficulty regarding your finances.

The amount of time you spend thinking about money, how you earn money, and how you spend or save money can tell you a great deal about your priorities, more than almost any other area of your life. Here are some additional questions to help you understand how you think about money.

Evaluate: Money and Your History

a. What were your family's attitudes towards money?

_____

_____

b. Who was the main provider in your family? _____

c. Did your family have financial problems?_____

d. Did they use a budget? _____

e. Did they fight over money? _____

f. Who managed the money?_____

g. Did someone control the money?_____

h. Did they go into debt? _____

    What for?_____

i. What did you learn from your family about money that was good?

_____

_____

j. What did you learn from your family about money that was not profitable?

_____

k. How was your experience with money different from your spouse? How is it alike or similar?

_____

_____

_____

l. How do you want to change or handle money in your own home? Discuss the above as well as other issues and establish your own plan.

_____

_____

_____

It will be beneficial to understand what your spouse's answers to these questions are. Ask them if they would take the time to respond to the questions above. If they will, have them write down their answers. Then compare your answers.

Take the information you learned earlier in the chapter and the answers to these questions and begin to consider a plan to help you move towards financial health in your home. You may need to call a financial planner to help you with this process

As you begin to develop a plan to improve your financial health, here is a list of some very basic money management principles:

1. A budget is a necessity. This is a joint project.
2. Establish a simple method of record keeping.

3. Work together toward common financial goals.

4. Decide how you will use credit and credit cards. Set limits.

5. Get out of debt.

6. Discontinue credit buying unless you know you can pay for it without paying the interest fee.

7. Think before buying.

8. Be very careful before you borrow money to invest. (This is to guard you against get rich quick schemes.)

9. Establish an emergency fund. (Define what is an emergency.)

10. Savings must be a fixed budget item.

11. Be open to changing your budget if necessary.

12. Prepare for the future.

I have included the following budget as an opportunity for you to fill in the numbers and find out where your money is going. Begin to keep your receipts and key in the data to start your budget.

The amount of $ you have left over after you have budgeted all of your monthly expenses gives you an idea of whether you are living within your means. Establish your budget and try using it for sixty days. After sixty days, readjust the numbers if you have to. Remember this is a beginning to help you gain financial peace to increase your wealth.

BUDGET FORM

GROSS INCOME PER MONTH .... $ _____

TAKE-HOME PAY .... $ _____

   1. HOUSING (Total) .... $ _____

       Mortgage/rent .... $ _____

       Insurance .... $ _____

       Taxes .... $ _____

       Electricity .... $ _____

       Gas .... $ _____

       Water .... $ _____

       Sanitation .... $ _____

       Telephone .... $ _____

       Maintenance .... $ _____

       Other .... $ _____

   2. FOOD (Total) .... $ _____

   3. AUTOMOBILES (Total) .... $ _____

       Payments .... $ _____

       Insurance .... $ _____

       Licenses/Taxes .... $ _____

       Maint./Repair/Replace .... $ _____

   4. INSURANCE (Total) .... $ _____

       Life .... $ _____

       Medical .... $ _____

   5. DEBTS (Total) .... $ _____

       Credit Card .... $ _____

       Loans and Notes .... $ _____

       Other .... $ _____

6. ENTERTAINMENT (Total) .... $ _____

    Eating Out .... $ _____

    Babysitters .... $ _____

    Activities/Trips .... $ _____

    Vacation/Recreation .... $ _____

7. CLOTHING (Total) .... $ _____

8. SAVINGS (Total) .... $ _____

9. MEDICAL EXPENSES (Total) .... $ _____

10. MISCELLANEOUS (Total) .... $ _____

    Toiletry, cosmetics .... $ _____

    Beauty, Barber .... $ _____

    Laundry, cleaning........................... $ _____

    Allowances, lunches .... $ _____

    Subscriptions .... $ _____

    Gifts (inc. Christmas) .... $ _____

11. SCHOOL/CHILDCARE (Total) ...... $ _____

    Tuition .... $ _____

    Materials .... $ _____

    Transportation .... $ _____

    Day Care .... $ _____

12. INVESTMENTS (Total) .... $ _____

TOTAL EXPENSES .... $ _____

TAKE-HOME PAY .... $ _____

AVAILABLE AFTER EXPENSES .... $ _____

Final Reflections

- Knowing how much money you have, how much your bills cost a month, and what you spend your money on will help you learn to rule over your money instead of it ruling you.

- Observing what you spend your money on and how much money you spend can help you make different choices.

- Keep a record of all the money you spend in a month. See where it goes. Is this what you want to spend your money on?

M – Money Needs To Be Handled With Care!

NO THREATS OR MANIPULATION

Having a successful marriage is all about honoring one another. Respecting your spouse's wishes and desires is very important. When you threaten one another it takes away the freedom of the other individual. Threats are usually communicated through meanness. Manipulation and threats just don't work.

When a person threatens another, they don't really need a great deal of understanding of the other person. They just need to know what the person likes or doesn't like, or what the person is afraid of. When a person threatens another, they don't really care how it affects the other, just whether they get their point across.

Sometimes people make very obvious threats that are clear and recognizable. Other times they threaten in ways that are hidden and very disrespectful to the other person. The offender is interested in the person they are attacking feeling great anxiety and like danger is imminent.

Manipulation

No one likes to be manipulated. It is another way of bulldozing over one another. When a person uses manipulation, just like with the use of threats, they must have some insight into the other person's likes and dislikes, strengths and vulnerable points. If threats and manipulation are a part of your marriage, it is time to end them. They will only bring harm.

Types of Threats and Manipulation

Here are some specific examples.

- **Seduction & Deception:** This is where a person hides or is deceitful with their actions. They say one thing, only to lure their spouse into what they wanted anyway. It can be as simple as ordering pizza or as complex as buying a new home. It is the opposite of honesty. It plays with their partner's emotions and will bring quick destruction to a marriage.

- **Martyrdom:** Their favorite line is, "Look what I have done for you." They hope to make their spouse feel guilty.

- **Dominance:** This looks like oppression — not respecting the wishes or desires of their spouse. Being controlling. Always getting their way.

- **Submission:** They submit to their spouse's desires or suggestions, but in submitting they really look like a martyr. They only submit to produce guilt and shame in their partner in order that they will end up getting what they wanted anyway. There is an appropriate submission to one another, but it involves love, respect and honor. We will say more about this under the letter Y.

- **Intimidation:** Overpowering their spouse. Being a bully. Taking advantage of their weakness and putting them into a place of fear.

Evaluate: Your Use of Threats and Manipulation

Take some time to reflect on how you have been treating your spouse.

Do you use threats in your marriage? _____

Do you manipulate them into doing what you want disregarding their desires? _____

Are any of the patterns listed above present in your marriage? _____

If you realize that you are threatening or manipulating your spouse it is time to put into action what you learned in chapter C under Confess. Go and get some help to change your ways. Ask them to confirm whether you are one who uses threats and manipulation to get what you want.

Call a friend, your counselor, a spiritual leader, someone who can help you change your behavior and ask them for help.

Evaluate: Your Spouse's Use of Threats and Manipulation
Now think about how you have been treated by your spouse.

Do they use threats in your marriage? _____.

Do they manipulate you into doing what they want disregarding your desires? _____

Do you let them threaten and manipulate you? _____

    If you realize that you are being threatened or manipulated by them it is also time to get some help. It has been said that if bitterness and resentment take root inside of you it will poison your entire body. Because of this reason it is also important that if you have received offenses and hurts from your spouse, they must be spoken about, addressed, and resolved. If not they will continue to cause problems in your marriage.

    If you are being threatened and manipulated in your relationship take a moment to write down what you are feeling.

_____

_____

_____

_____

_____

_____

List the statements or events that make you feel like you are being threatened or manipulated.

1. _____

   _____

2. _____

   _____

3. _____

   _____

4. _____

   _____

Share these with your spouse. Ask them if they will change or get some help. If they won't go for help, call someone to help give you wisdom on how to live with your spouse. Unless these behaviors stop in your marriage they will only increase in their intensity and quantity.

N – No Threats or Manipulation!

OPINIONS NEED TO BE SHARED WITH CARE

Your spouse needs to know that they are safe in your presence. When you share and when you listen, are you pursuing things that make for peace in your relationship? Let's consider the way that you resolve conflict, the way that you fight. Conflict resolution often means I'm right, you're wrong. If this is your definition, it is time for a change.

Peacemakers or Peace Lovers

There are those who love peace and those who are peacemakers. Those who love peace often give up their own ideas, plans, or what they want because peace is more enjoyable then any type of disagreement.

What I want to encourage is being a peacemaker. This is a person who is confident to enter into conflict and is wise enough to be able to express their own needs and wants. They are able to find a middle ground while making peace which respects their spouse and who they are. This is a skill that can be developed and will certainly help you in your marriage.

Different Need Systems

Conflict is primarily the intersecting of two need systems, the needs of one person colliding with the needs of the other. Many people bring neurotic needs into marriage. Neurotic needs are exaggerations of normal needs and they are usually ambivalent. On the conscious level the person desires one thing, on a non-conscious level just the opposite. That person is always frustrated because it is impossible for them to be satisfied.

Where there is a conflict of two needs or desires, one person's needs are more important than the other person's. If there is a great deal of emotion and you don't know what the root of the conflict is, understanding your spouse's feelings is going to be significantly more difficult.

When we are in conflict with our spouses, it is important that we allow ourselves to enter fully into their world of feelings and personal meanings and see things as they do. We step into their views so completely that we lose all desire to evaluate or judge them. We enter it so sensitively that we can respond freely to their feelings without trampling on them.

Negative Emotions

When you are listening to your spouse and you sense a negative emotion, it is helpful to know what is going on inside them. When they are depressed, know that inside of their depression there are often judgments they have made about themselves, a situation, or another. There is hopelessness and helplessness.

When they express grief, you'll often find hopes that have not come to pass. Some of these hopes might be realistic and others might be unrealistic. When they express their anger they are making a demand. This demand can either be just or unjust.

Finally, when they are expressing resentment, it is often because they are under an illusion that something should have been different.

These thoughts are detrimental to a healthy marriage. They need to be processed and healing needs to come.

What Does Resolving Conflict Mean?

Conflict resolution does not mean that we have to settle everything at the moment. It does not mean that we have to come to immediate conclusions. It is learning to give and to take. It often means coming to a middle ground.

When people come into my office and they are having continual conflicts, the first thing I encourage them to do is to monitor the kinds of conflicts in their life and see what happens in the conflict.

Consider how did the fight start? Two persons meet, begin to relate and eventually marry. Their interaction brings together the needs, problems, personality patterns, resources, expectations, and hopes of each other. Eventually, their interactions are not as peaceful as they were in the beginning.

Evaluate: What Do Your Fights Look Like?
Ask yourself these questions:

1. What are some things you do that your mate finds irritating?

   _____

   _____

   _____

2. Are there things you could do differently? _____

   _____

   _____

3. What happens in your relationship that causes bad feelings?

   _____

   _____

   _____

   _____

4. How does the fight start? _____

   _____

   _____

5. Then what happens? _____

   _____

   _____

6. What happens next? _____

_____

_____

7. How does it all end? _____

_____

_____

8. How do you feel afterward? _____

_____

_____

Replaying the Video

I use the example of replaying the video. Look at what happened and try to understand where the problem began and how it can be avoided the next time. Trying to figure out what happened is okay in a marriage if you are learning what went wrong in order that you can get it right the next time.

Handling Conflict

Howard Markman, in his book, *Fighting For Your Marriage* (San Francisco, Jossey-Bass Publishers, 1994), describes how most people handle conflict in one of four ways:

1. We must win.
2. We surrender and give up.
3. We withdraw or pull back saying this is not over yet.
4. We seek resolution, and try to find a way that we can live with our partner's opinion or behavior.

Obviously, #4 is the preferred method of handling conflict.

When I sit down with a couple when they are usually in the midst of conflict and it hasn't been resolved, my hope is that I can help them unblock their communication lines and communicate more effectively. I try to interrupt their pattern of mutual attack and retaliation.

Their conflict is often triggered by their frustration of not having their needs met. They are also frustrated that their efforts to reform their spouse aren't working. You may find yourself experiencing these same frustrations.

I want to help them become aware of the strengths and unused assets in themselves and in their relationship that can be used to make constructive changes in themselves and their marriage. I will help them identify specific areas where change or growth must occur. I will help them negotiate these areas and begin to work toward their completion. Hopefully, I will get to watch them experience the change together. When you find someone to help you resolve your conflict, hopefully that is what they will be doing.

Conflict Patterns

Markman also lists several ways people react to conflict. These patterns get them into a great deal of trouble. As you read these, which do you fall into? I have written them as if you are the one needing to change. You may quickly realize that your spouse also reacts one of these ways. As with every other piece of information you have learned so far, there will be benefit when you and your spouse talk about these patterns and partner together to change them into a better approach.

- **Pattern 1:** An increased escalation in volume and tone during the conflict. You start talking rather loudly and your spouse tries to talk louder or with more emotion. You then try to talk louder than your spouse and soon you are yelling and shouting. This may lead to physical violence.

- **Pattern 2:** You hear what your spouse says and you discount it. You act as if it's not important. You don't pay attention to what was said. You don't really listen to them and they don't hear you.

- **Pattern 3**: You simply withdraw and avoid the conflict. This is when, in the midst of an argument or conflict, you get up and leave your spouse either physically, emotionally, or both. You avoid what was said and don't revisit the topic. This usually touches abandonment issues in your spouse.

- **Pattern 4**: Because you have experienced so much from your spouse, no matter what they say or try to do, you don't believe they are serious. You believe they are just saying what they think they're supposed to say, but really there is no sincerity behind their words. You interpret your spouse's words negatively. I already talked about this in chapter B – under "Believing the Best."

Evaluate: What Do Your Conflicts Look Like?

Think about the last conflict you had. Was there a healthy resolution, or did you and your spouse fall into any of these patterns? If so, which pattern did you fall into?

Pattern 1. Escalation? _____

Pattern 2. Discounting? _____

Pattern 3. Withdrawal? _____

Pattern 4. Believing the worst? _____

If you handle conflict using any of these patterns, you will become increasingly frustrated.

Take a moment and identify two conflicts that are currently occurring in your marriage.

1. _____

_____

_____

2. _____

_____

_____

Go and ask your spouse what they think the current conflicts are in your marriage.

1. _____

   _____

   _____

2. _____

   _____

   _____

These conflicts must be discussed. It is important not to delay bringing them to resolution or it is going to be increasingly difficult to have a marriage that will last a lifetime.

Wisdom Regarding Sharing Your Opinions

Finally, here is some wisdom which should help you as you share your opinion in a way that will be heard and understood.

1. A soft answer often will help turn away an angry attack.

2. Give your response after you fully hear what your spouse is saying.

3. When the argument continues to increase it is wise to slow it down or stop until a calmer demeanor is presented.

4. Don't hold onto your anger regarding past hurts. Continue to respond gently, kindly and tenderly.

Hopefully you can begin to put into practice some of the ABC's that you have already read about in order to bring a peaceful resolution to your areas of conflict.

O – Opinions Need To Be Shared With Care!

PARENTING IS A TEAM ACTIVITY

I think they are your kids! Let's have some more. Having children is supposed to be a shared pleasure. Look again at some of the wisdom the Bible gives us regarding training them. Proverbs 22:6 says, "Train up a child in the way he should go, even when he is old he will not depart from it." Ephesians 6:4a says, "Fathers, do not provoke your children to anger." Colossians 3:21 says, "Fathers, do not exasperate your children, that they may not lose heart."

How are you teaching your children about money? Do your children honor you or your spouse? How are you disciplining your children? Do you have family devotions? Do your children help with the chores? How parents handle these areas are different for almost every family.

It is important to realize that children will control your life if you let them. They will monopolize every second of your time. They will control your sex life. They will divide and conquer. Raising children will be significantly easier if we understand these truths. You will either train your children or they will train you.

Wisdom Regarding Raising Your Children
The following wisdom principles will help you raise your children:

- You cannot live your life through your child. Just because you didn't accomplish a dream does not mean that your child can accomplish your unfulfilled dream.

- Today we often end up putting our children into too many activities. Be careful that your children have some free time of their own to play and be free to do what they want to do. Children need structure;

however, they also need a balance of free time playing by themselves at home. Taking time to play with your children is important.

- Sometimes parents want to be their child's best friend. It is important to have a friendship with your children but when being their friend gets in the way of parenting them, you must choose to be their parent instead of their friend. This will change, as your children become adults.

Since my children are now adults, I am finding them to be very good friends. However, when they were between the ages of zero and somewhere in the teens, I was very much their parent and also a friend to them.

Children need to know that each spouse values the relationship with their husband or wife before their children. I told my children that they would go on and live their own lives; however, I was planning on living with their mother for many years after they left home.

The Goals of Parenting

- One major goal of parenting is that our children will be able to live on their own successfully. We do all that we can to help them.

- To have a relationship with your children is another goal. If you want them to talk to you when they are teenagers, you must talk to them when they are between the ages of one and twelve. It is helpful if you are always respectful.

Establishing relationships with your children needs to be a priority as you help them mature. Playing games with your children is a great way to build relationships. There is a fine line between being competitive and letting them win. There was a time in our game playing when my children felt bad when they beat me at a game. Sometimes they wanted to let me win. When they would win, I would celebrate. I would tell them that my goal was that they would be better at everything than I was.

Your Children Sharing Your Values

When our son was growing up, one day he brought home a CD that had words on it that were not appropriate in our home. I was listening to the music from his room and quickly asked him what the band was singing about. He had no idea what they were saying. He just liked the music. I asked him to take the words that were on the inside sleeve and tell me what each song was about. I took the CD and told him when he was done with the assignment we would look at it together and talk about it.

It took him about three months to finish the paper I had asked him to prepare. When he was done, we talked about each song. He realized that the values in the music he was listening to were not his values or ours. I remember watching him take the CD and throw it into the trash.

As our son grew, his interest in music changed, and I am sure that he listened to music that didn't reflect the same values as his mother's and mine. However, at the age of eleven, a point was made without simply taking the CD away and telling him that he couldn't listen to that kind of music in our house. He was given a choice and an opportunity to process what he was doing, even at the age of eleven.

Children want to be respected. They also want to be treated as adults, even if they aren't.

Family Talks

Many families try to have a time of devotions during the week, a time when they talk about the values that are important in their lives and that are to be practiced in their home. These times can often be wonderful or very frustrating.

We began a practice when the children were very little that proved to be very helpful. We began to talk about the topics of the day and relate them to our values — things that happened at school, or things we saw at a movie or on TV that were consistent or not consistent with the values that my wife and I hoped our children would reflect would soon be topics for family devotions.

These times of discussion could happen any time. We didn't have to wait for Wednesday night to talk about important things. They became very important for helping to illustrate the values that were important in our home. These conversations gave the children an opportunity to consider what they believed.

What Do You Do About the Chores?

Another place of difficulty in raising children is getting them to do their chores. This often leads to an argument or disagreement about the chores leading you to ask the question, "How do we get our children to do their chores?"

Here are a few suggestions to avoid the chore wars.

1. Lower your standards. Be sure your expectations are age appropriate.
2. Be direct with your children.
3. Try not to use the phrase, you should. Usually it offends your child and doesn't help. Try to find another word than should. For example, why don't you, or have you considered, or what do you think about this, can help your child more fully understand. This is a way to enter into your child's world rather than lecturing them with should.
4. Be clear as you show and tell them how to do a specific chore.
5. After they have done the chore don't go back and redo it. Teach them to do it the way you want it done.
6. Consider listening to your child's opinion and compromising when appropriate.
7. If they don't do the chore, don't assume responsibility for their negligence. Remember, it is just a chore. Try to always strengthen the relationship.
8. Choose your battles.

What About Discipline?

Let's talk about discipline. It involves training and encouragement. It is not abuse or punishment. It is fair and expected. It upholds the dignity of the child. It is balanced, often painful, but leaves no scares. It is prompted by concern and leads to a respect for authority. It strengthens self-esteem.

What About Abuse?

Abuse, however, is unfair and often unexpected. It is degrading and demoralizing. It is often harsh and leaves scars. It creates terror and resentment and destroys self-esteem. Discipline is important for your children. Abuse is never to be used. Don't yell, scream, and flip out, when your children don't get it right. Let them try again. Let them keep practicing.

Learning to love your children is very important. They need a lot of love and affection. Normally children get too much correction. When correction is not couched in love, it kills the life in a child. It is far more important to be positive than to be negative. When you are talking with your children, at least four positive statements are needed to offset one negative statement.

What Do You Do When Your Children Get It Wrong?

When your son or daughter brings home a paper and they miss nine out of ten questions, there are several ways to handle this dilemma. You can rant and rave. You can tear up the paper. You can call the teacher and ask for a meeting. You can yell at your child and tell them how "stupid" they are — or you can take time to work with your child and try to help them do better the next time.

If you help them and the next time instead of missing nine of ten, they miss six of ten, you were able to help them improve. Your positive encouragement, "You can do this," or "It is going to be okay," is often much more beneficial, coupled with additional time spent helping them learn the material than ranting and raving and telling them how "dumb" they are.

Quality Time

There is a lot of emphasis in the world on quality time. I believe this is not totally accurate. Quantity time is important also. Just being present can be as important as quality time. Often the phrase quality time is only used as an excuse to allow us to lead our busy lives. Our children need to know that they are as important, if not more important, than our jobs.

The song, "Cats in the Cradle" by Harry Chapin, describes how a son learned from his father what was important. What his dad taught him is that family time is down the list of importance. When the son grew up and the dad wanted to be with him, just like the son had wanted to be with his dad years before, the son was too busy. At the end of the song, it is obvious that the dad wished he had taught his son the importance of family.

Considering How You Were Raised

It is important to evaluate how you were raised — to look at the ways that your parents treated you. Not that you judge them, but that you evaluate their ways with wisdom. Keep what is good and leave behind what was harmful.

As you try to gain wisdom for raising your family, you can ask your friends what is working in their family. As you and your spouse consider what you want for your children, make a plan how you can help them grow up to be responsible adults.

When our children were younger, Reneé gave more attention helping them grow up. She was at home more with them while I was gone during the day. As our children became older, I got more involved in raising the children.

Often fathers think that they are baby-sitting their children when they are with them. Father's don't baby-sit their children. It is called parenting.

Moms Need a Break Also

Moms also need to have breaks from their children so that they can get refreshed. There was a time in our first few years of marriage that Reneé and I realized that she needed some time away from the family where she could develop relationships with some of her friends and have time for herself. I decided to stay at home and watch my children while she went out and had a good time. From this experience, I was more aware how tiring and exhausting it was to care for our children.

A danger for moms is that they have to be superwoman. They want to, or they feel the need to be working in the marketplace, and taking care of their family. Some mothers don't want to be working in the market-place; they would rather stay at home. Mothers need to be free to choose to do whatever is needed for each season of their lives.

Children Need Their Parents

It is important for you to know that your children need you. Some-times you have to make a choice to not earn as much money, to not climb as high in the corporate world so that you can be more focused on being with your family. It is a difficult balance to try to earn enough money to do the things you want and need to do in your life and to also find the necessary time to be with members of your family.

Right now, take some time to consider the amount of time you are currently spending interacting with your wife or husband and with your children during a typical week. The number of hours, or lack of, might surprise you.

Hours spent with my wife/husband in a week? _____

Hours spent with each child in a week? (List each child separately.)

         Child's name: Time spent together:

_____   _____

_____   _____

_____   _____

In order for you and your spouse to be in unity, you must come into agreement regarding how you are going to raise your children. When the plan is not working, adjust it. Evaluate what is working and what isn't working. Don't wait five years down the road until the damage is done. To be in unity with your spouse is powerful. When you are in disunity, it creates havoc. This does not mean that you always have to have the same opinion. It does mean that you have discussed the issue and decided together what course of action you are going to pursue.

We learned a lot from Dr. James Dobson while raising our children. He helped us have a sense of humor regarding them. Reading books on child development helped us know what you can expect from a child at a certain age. Knowing when to discipline and when not to discipline is important. Disciplining rebellion is different than training a child who is simply growing up.

Parenting Keys

Here is a list that I hope helps you:

- Be consistent.

- Let your yes be yes and your no be no.

- Discuss with your children when it is appropriate to ask questions.
- Follow through, and keep your word.
- If you don't know your answer when asked a question, tell your children you will think about it, discuss it with your spouse, and get back to them later.
- If you are wrong, admit it and ask for forgiveness.
- Too much control can prolong your child's maturing.
- Be united in your decisions and disciplines.

Parenting Is About Relationship

Involvement is different than control. Involvement is being present, giving oversight and direction while your children enjoy doing things they have chosen to do with your permission. Control is dictating your child's every thought, word, and action.

Parenting is about relationship. Your children will learn how to respect, honor, and love you and others by the way you respect, honor, and love them. Relationship takes involvement in your child's life.

What Do You Do When You Disagree With Your Spouse?

Discuss things you disagree about with your spouse in private. Children do not enjoy watching their parents fight. It is not their business. They need to know that you disagree, but there are limits on how much they see, watch and listen to.

If you and your spouse don't agree, after much discussion, prayer, and time, and a decision must be made, it is important that each spouse supports the other. Once you make the decision, you agree to stand together, respecting and encouraging one another. United you stand, divided you fall. And when it doesn't go the way you thought it should, the spouse that wasn't in agreement doesn't say, "I told you so."

In our home sometimes I defer to Reneé's opinion and wisdom; other times she defers to me. When times regarding our children came that we couldn't come to agreement, I was the one who usually made the final decision. This happened only a few times in our marriage.

My wife trusted me to make the decision. In some marriages this isn't possible because spouses don't trust one another. Reneé's trust in me has been earned over the years through her watching me handle situations that made her feel safe and secure.

If after a time the plan that you and your spouse agreed upon isn't working, regroup, make a new plan and try it again. It is important that you both are in agreement walking out the new plan together. Remember you and your spouse are on the same team.

Evaluate: Where Are Your Children Causing Difficulty?

The exercise for this chapter is to identify those places regarding your children that are currently causing difficulty.

Describe the situation that needs to be addressed.

1. _____

_____

_____

2. _____

_____

_____

3. _____

_____

_____

As you have done in the past, these areas need to be talked about with your spouse. Find out whether they agree that these are areas that need help. Ask them to identify the areas that are concerns for them. They can write them on the following spaces.

1. _____

_____

_____

_____

2. _____

_____

_____

_____

3. _____

_____

_____

_____

Once you have come to agreement on these issues begin to try to resolve them using the ABC principles that have already been discussed.

P – Parenting Is a Team Activity!

P

Q
QUICKLY MAKE PEACE

Often when I meet with a couple and they begin to really look at the areas of difficulty in their relationship, wounds are uncovered that were inflicted by each other months and years ago. Many times the offense or hurt happened as early as the wedding night, or even before their marriage. Because they don't like confrontation or they might not even have been aware they were hurt, they don't talk about it. The offense was never made right.

What happens is that the offense doesn't go away. It begins to impact how they relate. It becomes one of the reasons that people don't always believe the best about their spouse. The hurt becomes like an infected sore. It may scab over but will still be tender to the touch. It probably will get infected again and be even worse. It is important to deal with these wounds quickly.

When offenses are not dealt with immediately, they often become more significant than if they would have been addressed when the event happened. It is not uncommon that the event actually looks worse months or years later. I encourage them to take time to talk about what happened so that each partner understands how they were hurt, or how they hurt each other.

What About When You've Been Wounded Many Times?

When your spouse hurts or offends you, it is normal for you to have difficulty forgiving them and even forgetting about it. If you are a person who has been wounded many times, you may need to see some proof whether they are really sorry.

It is necessary when you get hurt to have your spouse tell you they are sorry and to ask you to forgive them. It is also important for you to tell your spouse you are sorry and ask them to forgive you when you hurt or offend them. You need to go to them quickly and apologize and try to make it right.

Just because they forgive you does not automatically mean that they will be able to trust you right away. Just because you forgive them does not automatically mean that you will also be able to trust them immediately.

Evaluate: Places of Hurt That Need To Be Made Right

Think for a moment if there are areas in your life that are places of hurt where you did not have your spouse make peace with you. If they still hurt, write them on the following lines.

1. _____

_____

_____

2. _____

_____

_____

3. _____

_____

_____

4. _____

_____

_____

Q

The next step will be to share these with your spouse seeking to make peace. There is a good chance they won't even know they hurt you.

Think if there are places you have hurt your spouse that you need to make right. If you can't think of any go and ask them. Then take time to list them.

1. _____

_____

2. _____

_____

3. _____

_____

After you have made your list, go to them and tell them you are sorry and ask them to forgive you.

There will be times when you or your spouse will be offended or hurt and you are able to let it go. You are not bothered by it. Then there are times when neither of you can let the hurt go. These are the times when you go to another and get help to settle the issue quickly.

If this principle becomes a part of your marital lifestyle, your lives will be well on the way to a fulfilling, nurtured marriage.

Q – Quickly Make Peace!

RELATIONSHIPS NEED CLEAR BOUNDARIES

What often happens in a marriage is that the man or woman is too connected to their family or friends, and complications follow. Often one family has too much input into the married couples life, and it begins to create division between the couple.

There are different seasons of life that will require different family boundaries. For example, if you are required to care for your parents, you must have some very specific parameters. If you need to live with one of your families for a while, boundaries also need to be clearly established.

Some families find it difficult to let go of their children as they become adults and marry. Your family may perceive your marriage as a loss for them. They may feel like they have lost you and that things won't ever be the same. On the other hand, they might view your marriage as bringing another member into their family. Either one of these ideas can provide the environment for good or bad things to occur.

Evaluate: Questions To Gain Perspective

• What do you call your in-laws? _____

• How do you celebrate your upcoming holidays ... at your house or at one of your parents?

_____

Which parent? _____

• Do any relatives or friends have concerns about your marriage? _____

Which ones? _____

R

- Does your family respect the decisions you make? _____

- Do you enjoy being with your relatives? _____

- Do you enjoy being with your spouse's relatives? _____

- Do you enjoy being with your spouse's friends? _____

- Can your parents or family give you financial assistance and it be okay?

  _____

- Are your family members or friends causing problems in your marriage?

  _____

  Identify the family member that is causing problems in your marriage?

  _____

- Is it okay that your spouse is with his/her family so much? _____

  If any of these items are a concern to you, they must be discussed and resolved.

Have your spouse answer these same questions.

- What do you call your in-laws? _____

- How do you celebrate your upcoming holiday s ... at your house or at one of your parents?

  _____

  Which parent? _____

- Do any relatives or friends have concerns about your marriage? _____

  Which ones? _____

- Does your family respect the decisions you make? _____

- Do you enjoy being with your relatives? _____

146

- Do you enjoy being with your spouse's relatives? _____

- Do you enjoy being with your spouse's friends? _____

- Can your parents or family give you financial assistance and it be okay?

  _____

- Are your family members or friends causing problems in your marriage?

  _____

  Identify the family member that is causing problems in your marriage?

  _____

- Is it okay that your spouse is with his/her family so much? _____

There are no absolute answers to the questions above. Your marriage will be unique in the answers that you give. It is important concerning your family and friend relationships that you continue to put into practice the basic ABCs that you have begun to learn about in this book. Remember, it is always about love, honor and respect. You and your spouse need to have the same understanding regarding relationships with friends and relatives.

Holiday Wisdom

When you go to visit your family it is important that you balance the times of being alone as your family unit with visiting your family and friends. You may need to have your family or friends come and visit you instead of you doing all the traveling.

It is important that you also have time alone with your immediate family in order that you can begin to create your own family traditions. Try to find the balance between visiting your extended family and friends on holidays, and being together with your own family.

Some people have the morning to mid-afternoon of holidays for themselves and then see extended family in the evening. Some people visit with their family the week before or after a holiday, or the day before or after the holiday. It is important to think this through. Every season of life will be different.

Evaluate: Family and Friends' Concerns

Identify areas of concern where you feel like either your family or friends, or your spouse's family or friends, have too much input into your marriage.

1. _____

_____

_____

2. _____

_____

_____

3. _____

_____

_____

As always, the items you have listed need to be discussed. If you are to continue to nurture your marriage in this relationship, it is very important to know that you are on the same page with your spouse.

Now take a moment and write how you could help solve these problems.

1. _____

_____

_____

2. _____

_____

_____

3. _____

_____

_____

Finally, identify changes that would improve your family relationships (your spouse's or your family). If you think there needs to be healthier boundaries in your relationships with family members, take time now to identify them.

1. _____

_____

_____

2. _____

_____

_____

3. _____

_____

_____

As your own family unit, you need to decide what is best for you. Look at the items that you have written down and make an action plan with your spouse to begin to address them.

It is quite common for family and friends to be problems for marriages. With some discussion, a plan, and putting it into action, you can work toward more peaceful relationships.

R – Relationships Need Clear Boundaries!

SEX IS FOR MARRIAGE

It is surprising how little is known about lovemaking in marriage. Most couples know about having sex, but not about making love. Making love is supposed to be fabulous. Not too long ago, having sex was justified only as a means of procreation. Today, we can decide when we want to have children and how many we can provide for. We can choose to have foreplay and lovemaking for intimate bonding and fun. We can enjoy the whole sexual process for recreation and the enhancement of intimacy.

Reasons God Created Sex

I believe that God created everything, including the ability for men and woman to have sex. There are some very obvious reasons why God created sex. The most obvious is so that babies can be born. Even though babies can now be conceived using test tubes, they still need the union of a sperm and an egg. This is possible because God created male and female.

When you have sex with your spouse, you have the possibility of knowing them like no one else. Having sex links them to you in a way that was only meant for a husband and wife relationship. You are able to understand them like no one else in the world. It is part of the beauty that marriage reflects. Making love and experiencing sexual intercourse is supposed to give you pleasure. For many couples this is not true. It has often been said that when making love works, there is nothing better. But if it doesn't work, there is nothing worse.

If you are able to make love to your spouse and it is pleasurable, it can help guard you from an affair. It can help keep you from pornography and from adultery. However, just because you are having great lovemaking with your spouse is not a guarantee that you won't have an affair or use pornography.

Making love is supposed to bring comfort, relaxation, and rest. For many couples, having sex does just the opposite. Instead of it being a place of enjoyment, it is a place that brings great pain.

Healthy lovemaking helps defuse negative emotions and behaviors. Spouses who experience sexual intimacy are connected in a way that those who don't have it can't understand.

Reasons Why Romance Doesn't Happen

- We are too busy.

- We have no plan.

- We have inhibitions.

- We are not knowledgeable.

- We have unresolved hurts and tensions in our marriage.

- We are exhausted from raising our children.

- We start making love too late at night.

- We are not comfortable to talk about what we need regarding our sexual needs. We don't share what we like during lovemaking and then we long for it.

- We think that our partner will be offended and reject us.

- We do not take the time daily to connect emotionally.

- We have a physical or hormonal problem.

The Difference Between Having Sex and Making Love

I would like to explain the difference between having sex and making love. Sex is the intimate physical act of intercourse. Making love involves how you treat one another from the time you wake up until the time you have sex, and go to bed. This involves the attitudes you have toward one another, how you encourage, communicate and help them. Making love is an art that takes a lifetime to practice and learn. It is about honor, love, and respect.

Honor means to regard with outward respect. Love is affection based on admiration or benevolence, charity, warm attachment, enthusiasm, devotion and unselfish concern that freely accepts another in loyalty. Respect is an act of giving particular consideration to and showing high or special regard for someone. Your words, attitudes, and actions help you to connect or disconnect emotionally, physically, and spiritually with your spouse.

Evaluate: Honor, Love, and Respect While Making Love

Share heart to heart. Think about making love with your spouse. I feel honored, loved, or respected by my spouse when they:

1. _____

_____

_____

2. _____

_____

_____

3. _____

_____

_____

What can I do to make them feel honored, loved, or respected?

1. _____

_____

_____

2. _____

_____

_____

3. _____

_____

_____

Now that you are finished, ask your spouse to answer this same question. When she is done, ask her if you can share the lists with each other.

Evaluate: Honor, Love, and Respect While Making Love

Think about making love with your spouse. I feel honored, loved, or respected by my spouse when they:

1. _____

_____

_____

2. _____

_____

_____

3. _____

_____

_____

Making love is enhanced as you think about giving pleasure to your spouse. When you know how they feel honored, loved and respected you have taken a giant step toward a more fulfilling sexual relationship. It is okay to talk about what you enjoy and even describe what is pleasurable and not pleasurable while making love. It will help you and your spouse love one another.

What's Permissible When It Comes to Sex?

There have been different ideas about what is permissible between a married couple when they are making love. There is debate about whether certain positions or techniques are appropriate. If the guidelines of love, honor and respect are in place, it is possible that different positions, techniques and styles can be tried and enjoyed.

Some couples may choose not to engage in certain expressions. We must be considerate and gentle with our spouses. Never should we do anything that violates their own being or offends them sexually. Making love is not about intercourse, oral sex, or any other specific technique. It is about experiencing one-flesh companionship. It is about loving one another. Respecting your spouse's boundaries is crucial.

Suggestions for a Successful Sexual Life

Having a successful sexual life is about learning to be a great lover. Here are some suggestions that will help you.

- Enjoy playfulness, the ability to let go of control so that you can try new behaviors, and have fun.

- Be knowledgeable. Study your mate's responses to know what is most enjoyable. Ask your spouse what they like and want.

- Know your own body and teach your spouse what turns you on and increases your desire. Also have some knowledge about technique.

- Be creative in your romance. This may include surprise gifts, foot and leg massages, mutual showers, candle light dinners.

- Exercise discipline. When you make love don't hesitate to lock the door to keep from getting interrupted. It is important to go to bed at the same time. It is okay to actually plan making love into your schedule. It is just as important and valid as being spontaneous.

- Learn to minimize the environmental distractions. Regarding children, enforce their bedtimes and teach them to respect a locked door.

The more you love, honor, and respect one another in a proper way, the more you will make love. These three actions create a desire to respond. They open the door for a more passionate lovemaking experience. This can also be your experience.

How To Create More Pleasure When Making Love

In a loving relationship, your sexuality is the gift that you give willingly. If you are too fatigued, busy or inhibited to have sexual relations regularly, you are missing part of the design of marriage. There are times when you will focus on satisfying your own needs and other times when you focus on satisfying your partner's needs. For example, consider orgasms; your mate does not experience your orgasm. You focus on your sexual feelings and allow them to build to a climax; this is hopefully an intensely personal and pleasurable experience. You purposely let your mind enjoy the intensity of your excitement.

Some people can't allow themselves to focus on themselves in this area of marriage, and yet it is a part of a vibrant sexual relationship. Your mate enjoys watching how much pleasure this brings to you, and your personal excitement arouses them. Sex is a means to an end and never an end in itself. Making love unites and excites, but without relationship it loses its dynamic appeal.

Mutual Pleasuring

Enjoying mutual pleasuring that is slow, without pressure and demands is critical to a truly intimate, nurturing and exciting sex life. Here are some guidelines.

- Coercing your spouse into behaviors you may find exciting but offends them is out of the question.

- Any sexual behavior outside of making love with your spouse that becomes a habit can rob you from enjoyment with them.

- During any type of sexual pleasuring, you must guard your fantasy and thought life. Thinking about another person while you are making love to your spouse is not beneficial in deepening intimacy. If this is the only way you can make love, it is time to see a counselor for help.

Kissing Is Halfway There

Dr. James Dobson mentions, in *Love for a Lifetime*,[1] a description of how a person gets from noticing someone to making love to them. The progression looks like this:

1. You notice them across the room.
2. Your eye catches their eye.
3. You speak to one another.
4. You take their hand.
5. You put your hand on their shoulder.
6. You then put your hand around their waist.
7. You face them.
8. You kiss them.
9. You put your hand on their head.
10. You touch their body.
11. You kiss their body.
12. You touch below the waist.
13. You have intercourse.

There is a way to move through this list that will benefit your lovemaking. If you go too quickly to number thirteen, you will not be attending to your spouse in a way that will nurture them in the best fashion. Kissing your spouse is over halfway there. There is something very powerful about kissing. It connects you to the other person in a way that is very intimate.

Three Levels

Parts of your body respond differently to touch. There are three levels.

• **Level three** areas are less sexual in nature, but capable of producing sensual arousal and sexual excitement. This includes the whole body, skin and nerve endings.

• **Level two** areas include the parts of the body that are normally stimulated during foreplay. The back of the knees, the inner thighs, the armpits, the breast, the abdomen, the navel, the small of the back, the neck from back to front, the eyelids, the edges of the nose, the temples, the mouth and tongue.

• **Level one** areas are the nipples and the genitals.

Level one should not be the immediate focus of making love. It is important to understand these levels. Often men will go right to level one without stopping for a while at levels three and two. If you are going to nurture your spouse in the area of sexuality, it will be important for you to visit levels two and three often, even more than you pursue level one.

Four Phases in Lovemaking

It is also important to understand that there are four phases in lovemaking. The phases are:

• The excitement phase
• The plateau phase
• The orgasm phase
• The resolution phase.

They are usually different for men and women. For many men, making love could be synonymous with the Minute Waltz. In other words, the whole "love dance" could take a very short time. However, for most women, it would be more like an entire symphony by Mozart. It is beneficial if spouses understand their partner's different phase. The excitement phase for a man might happen for just a few minutes, almost bypassing the plateau phase and leading quickly to orgasm.

And yet for the woman the first two stages might take 30-40 minutes or longer. If the man quits after he has had his ejaculation, he will probably leave his wife very frustrated. A woman might experience more than one orgasm. It is helpful for a husband to know this so that he can pleasure his wife.

There are ways for men to learn to control a quick ejaculation and hold it longer. This will also help them pleasure their wives for a longer period of time.[2]

Finally, the resolution phase for many women could take a half-hour or longer. However, for many men, they will just naturally fall asleep after intercourse.

Sometimes making love can happen in a very short time. For most, this is not usually the desired method of lovemaking. However, it is one of the ways you and your spouse can make love, especially if it is pleasurable to both of you.

If you know your spouse's phase and how they enjoy being pleasured by you, and if they know the same about you, you will experience more sexual pleasure. As with the other ideas in this book, try one or two of these and see if it will help you.

A Word About Pornography

Pornography can be extremely damaging to a relationship. It robs the thoughts and emotions that are meant for the spouse alone. Pornography can become like an affair. No one can compete with pornographic pictures of perfect physiques of men and women that are often airbrushed to look more sensual. Pornography is not real. It is a fantasy.

Evaluate: Making Love

Identify two things that are most pleasurable to you when you are making love with your spouse.

1.

2. _____

_____

Identify two things that are not pleasurable to you when you are making love with your spouse.

1. _____

_____

2. _____

Finally describe those areas that need some help and attention in your marriage regarding the sexual area.

1. _____

_____

2. _____

_____

Ask your spouse to do this same exercise and when they are done share your lists.

Identify two things that are most pleasurable to you when you are making love with your spouse.

1. _____

_____

2. _____

_____

Identify two things that are not pleasurable to you when you are making love with your spouse.

1. _____

_____

2. _____

_____

Finally describe those areas that need some help and attention in your marriage regarding the sexual area.

1. _____

_____

2. _____

_____

If you are not able to discuss these very intimate issues in a constructive way, it is time for you to get help from someone who has some expertise in helping people with these areas. The usual resources for help are your spiritual leader, a therapist or a counselor.

Nurturing your marriage sexually is one of the most important areas to care for in your life with your spouse.

S — Sex Is For Marriage!

[1] Dr. James C. Dobson, *Love For A Lifetime* (Portland, Oregon: Multnomah Press, 1987), pp. 32-34. Used by permission.

[2] Dr. Douglas E. Rosenau, *A Celebration of Sex* (Nashville, Tennessee: Thomas Nelson, Inc., 1994). This book is a good resource for helping men and women.

TRUST IS A FOUNDATIONAL PRINCIPLE

Another key to having a marriage that will last a lifetime is keeping your word. If you say you are going to do something, it is very important that you follow through. If you don't keep your word, your spouse won't know whether they can believe you or not. Trust will begin to be questioned, and this will lead to frustration on your spouse's part. They will feel like they can't depend on you to do what you said you would do, which will lead to bitterness and anger.

It isn't just about being faithful in your marriage and not flirting or having an affair with someone, which are obvious marriage killers. It is as simple as taking your spouse out for an evening that you had planned, coming home for supper at the time agreed upon, or picking up the milk and eggs at the store which you told them you would do. These actions help build trust.

Marriage Is Keeping Covenant

The word covenant is not often used with marriage in today's society. However, a marriage agreement is a covenant between two people. It is a promise to do the things you said you were going to do. In years past these are some of the basic elements of covenant:

- A binding, solemn agreement between two or more parties (not just a legal contract).

- In a covenant, the stronger helps the other where the other is weak or lacking.

- It is not dissolved by a change in feeling or on a whim, but is meant to be permanent.

- In a covenant, we risk who we are with someone else.

If you practice keeping your marriage covenant, you won't have any problem being believed or having your spouse trust you.

The Wedding Day

Think for a minute about the wedding day. Picture the groom with his hair combed perfectly, his tuxedo pressed and looking sharp, and the look on his face one of amazement as he awaits the woman he loves. Then she appears. She is dressed like a majestic queen with her veil and long white train as she marches down the aisle with all eyes gazing upon her. She is stunning.

The day before the wedding both the bride and groom were dressed in shorts and t-shirts. They even argued a little trying to finish the last details. But on the wedding day their appearance looks far different. They are dressed to reflect the beauty and splendor that is to come when two separate lives merge into one.

The Vows

Then they declare their love in the vows:

- I take you; the one they have chosen is unique.
- To be my wife/husband; the marriage is not a performance contract. It is built on love, tenderness and relationship.
- To have and to hold; they are each owned by the other in a very special way. They belong to no one else.
- From this day forward, for better, for worse, for richer, for poorer, in sickness and in health, to love and to cherish till death do us part. It's for a lifetime.
- According to God's holy law; God is a part of the process and joins the partners.
- And this is my solemn vow. They give their word, their promise, and all of their being.

Do you remember your wedding vows? _____

Is your heart fixed on fulfilling them?_____

What Do You Do If You Have Been a Liar?

If you have been a liar or have been unfaithful in your marriage, it is not impossible to rebuild trust; however, it is difficult. If you are the spouse who is having trouble being believed, here are some ways that you can help your spouse trust you again.

Ways To Build Trust

- You share your secrets with your spouse.
- You risk your most personal self because you know you are safe in your relationship.
- You show your spouse acceptance and forgiveness.
- You share with your spouse the feeling of how comfortable you are with them, the inexpressible joy of feeling at home with them, knowing that you are safe enough that you don't have to measure words nor mince phrases.
- You express total loyalty to your spouse in words and actions.
- You honor your spouse in public and private.
- You choose to live totally, sexually faithful.
- You are committed to truthful communication.

What Do You Do If You've Been Lied To?

If you have been the one who has been lied to, it is important that you are able to trust again.

Here are the steps to follow.

- Tell them that you don't trust them.
- Tell them why.
- Let them know it will take time to trust them again.
- Set some boundaries in your life, which can't be removed.

Don't allow yourself to be run over any longer. If they continue to lie to you and these first four points have not helped, you probably need to consider a counselor to help you get through this. Ask yourself if you trust your spouse. If the answer is no, then it is time to begin to try to rebuild trust in your relationship.

Evaluate: Places Where You Can't Trust Your Spouse

Identify the areas where you have felt betrayed and have difficulty trusting them.

1. _____

_____

_____

2. _____

_____

_____

3. _____

_____

_____

You will need to share these with them, putting into use the principles of the ABCs. If you can't communicate with one another in peace and understanding, you probably will need to get a mediator.

Evaluate: Where You Can't Be Trusted

If you are the one that can't be trusted, it is time to ask your spouse how you can rectify the situation. Ask them if they have felt betrayed and if they have difficulty trusting you. Have them write down those places where they have been hurt, in order that you can begin to change your behavior.

1. _____

_____

_____

2. _____

_____

_____

3. _____

_____

_____

4. _____

_____

_____

Being trustworthy and being able to trust your spouse are primary ingredients in having a marriage that will last a lifetime. As we near the conclusion of this book so many of these ABCs are absolutely crucial to your marriage being nurtured.

T – Trust Is a Foundational Principle!

UNDERSTANDING LEADS TO LOVE

Understanding your spouse is a lifetime process not accomplished in a month or even a year. Sometimes it may seem overwhelming. Being aware of the differences between you and your spouse will help you find solutions more quickly when you have conflicts. Being different doesn't mean that one is better than the other, or that one is right or wrong. You're just different.

My hope is that as you become more aware and have more understanding you will fall deeper in love with your spouse. Here is a list of differences between men and women that I have become aware of over the years. These are statements made in a general context and might not describe you.

Differences

Men:

- Age earlier, but wrinkle later.
- Lose weight more easily than women do.
- Talk about themselves less, but worry about themselves more.
- Need to feel respected, and to have their egos stroked as they are told what great providers they are.
- They usually take risks more easily. Example: living with no disability insurance is easier for a man than for a woman.
- Are often one track; for example, they can't talk and watch television at the same time.
- Enjoy leading and providing, but insist on it being their own way.

- Sit on feelings or lack the skills to express them.
- They tune in more visually to sexual cues and like to touch what they see and enjoy in their wife's body.
- They need little or no preparation for sex.
- They usually do not have their spouse's awareness of what the relationship should be like.
- Their only education for marriage may be the example they observed in their home.

Women:

- Generally need to feel secure as their safety and emotional needs are met.
- Do not take risks as readily.
- Want to feel connected and included.
- Want to be nurtured and protected.
- Are often freer in expressing emotions.
- Tune in visually to the whole person rather than just sexuality.
- Outlive men by four to eight years in the United States.
- Their sexual drive tends to be related to their menstrual cycle (while a man's drive is fairly constant).
- Are stimulated more by touch and romantic words.
- Are far more attracted by a man's personality while the man is stimulated by sight.
- Have a greater intuitive awareness of how to develop a loving relationship.
- Are initially more considerate of feelings and enthusiastic about developing a meaningful, multilevel relationship; she wants to be a lover, a best friend, a fan, and homemaker.
- Need to feel they are valuable to their husband, more important than his mother, his children, his friends, his secretary, and his job.
- Need to know that their husband is willing to share an intimate moment of comfort without demanding explanations or giving lectures.
- Need open and unobstructed communication.

- Need to be praised, need to feel free to help their husband without fearing retaliation and anger.
- Need to know that their husband will defend and protect them.
- Need to know their opinion is valuable.
- Need their husband to be the kind of man their son can follow and their daughter could marry.
- Need to share their life with their husband.
- Need to be tenderly held often, just to be near her husband, apart from times of sexual intimacy.
- Often need hours of emotional and mental preparation before having sex.

More Differences Between Men and Women

Often women tend to be more personal than men. Women have a deeper interest in people and feelings, and in building relationships, while men tend to be more preoccupied with practical things. Men tend to be more conquer oriented, competing for dominance, hence their strong interest in sports.

Often when a husband and wife travel together on a long trip they have different agendas. Gary Smalley describes the male as wanting to conquer the 400 miles; the female, however, wants to stop and shop and drink coffee. This interferes with the husband's goal of conquering the 400 miles.

A woman becomes an intimate part of the people they know and the things that surround them. They enter into a kind of oneness with their environment.

A man relates to people and situations, and he somehow remains apart. Women tend to find their identity in close relationships, while men gain their identity through vocations. Women need more time to adjust to change. A man can logically deduce the benefits of a change and get "psyched-up" for it in a matter of minutes. Women tend to express their hostility verbally, whereas men tend to be more physically violent.

Even the courtship is different for men. A man will pursue and charm a woman to win her; after winning her he feels that he has conquered her.

In a very real sense a man is filled up when he marries because his wife is now part of him. He is satisfied and has a tendency to look for other potential frontiers. If a man does not get a broader perspective than marriage being something he conquers, it will harm his marriage.

Women's magazines often deal with relationships and matters related to the family and to the home, such as sex, food, fashions, furnishings and marriage. Men's magazines reflect what men are interested in. This often involves sports, cars, physical fitness, and fixing up the home. Men enjoy stories about war, adventure, business dealings, traveling, money, and of course sex.

Men are into things and doing. Women are usually into people and being. Usually men, more than women, need time to think. They need to withdraw before they can reenter the conflict.

A young girl's impulse is to talk without thinking. A young boy's impulse is to act without thinking. Have you ever noticed why a man paces back and forth when a woman does not? He has to be doing something. A man usually must think about his feelings before he talks about them. A woman can usually feel, talk, and think all at the same time. A woman longs for a man to listen without getting bent out of shape or trying to fix her. She wants him to help her process what is going on.

Sex for a man usually does not have to involve relationship. Rather, for a man, sex often can include simply visual orientation. A man can be stimulated by a picture of a nude woman, and yet have no idea what type of person she is. This is one reason why men are so attracted to pornography. Remember, pornography is a marriage killer.

Let's Just Fix Them

A man comes home for the day, and his wife begins to tell him all the things that went wrong. Now maybe some of what she said is totally accurate and some isn't; however, most men's first response is to try to fix, or bring a solution to the problem. Guess what, she probably is not looking for him to solve her problem; rather, she is looking for him to hear her heart and simply listen to her. The husband trying to fix the situation actually only makes it worse.

Some men say: Women are too emotional, they don't feel the pressure to provide, they talk too much, they frequently deny their real power, and they try to change me. Some women say: Men aren't sensitive enough, they don't do their fair share of housework, they are afraid to be vulnerable or out of control, and they don't listen.

Nothing Better Than a Good Marriage

It has been said that there is nothing in the world better than a good marriage; unfortunately, there is often nothing worse than a bad marriage. Love convinces a couple that they have the greatest romance that has ever been, that no two people have loved as they love. Marriage is the down-to-earth dimension of romance. It is the closest bond possible between two human beings.

Just Like Us

When we think about the differences in our spouses, often we wish that they could be just like us. At times, we even despise their differences. Henry Higgins says in *My Fair Lady*, "Why can't a woman be more like a man?" He was trying to understand her.

There is the joke about a man who was walking on the beach and kicked up a bottle and a genie popped out. The genie quickly said, "Make a wish and it will be yours." The man thought for a couple of minutes and said, "I want you to build me a bridge to Hawaii, because I have always wanted to see Hawaii. I am afraid to fly and I don't like boats, and I really want to drive."

The genie said, "That sounds like a pretty hard request, think of all the concrete. Is there another wish that you have?"

The man thought for a while and said, "Okay, I want to be able to understand women."

The genie quickly said, "Two lanes or four."

Men and women often say, "I can't understand my spouse." Well, that is no longer an option. Your marriage will not work if you stay stuck in that opinion. This is a lie and we need to call it by its name, a lie. You can learn to understand your wife. You can learn to understand your husband.

Evaluate: Ways You and Your Spouse Are Different

Identify several ways you are different from your spouse.

1. _____

_____

_____

2. _____

_____

_____

3. _____

_____

_____

Remember, understanding almost always leads to love. Knowing the differences between you and your spouse will help you in your marriage.

Evaluate: Things You Don't Understand About Them

Make a list of things you don't understand about your spouse and would like to understand.

1. _____

_____

_____

2. _____

_____

_____

3. _____

_____

Now, take this list and ask your spouse to help you understand them.

Ask your spouse to write some of what they don't understand about you and what they would like too understand. When they are finished, have them share it with you.

1. _____

_____

_____

2. _____

_____

_____

3. _____

_____

_____

I have mentioned the old adage about climbing a mountain previously. It is true here also. The question is, "How do you climb a mountain?" The answer is, "One step at a time." So ... read, reflect, choose one or two of the many suggestions in this book that seem to touch your heart and focus on those rather than trying to do it all at one time.

It is possible to understand your spouse. It is also possible for them to understand you. Don't give up. Keep trying to learn how to nurture and build them up.

U – Understanding Leads to Love!

VACATIONS ARE IMPORTANT

I am writing this chapter on my return to Kansas after enjoying a relaxing vacation with my wife. It is not uncommon for me to meet with couples that have never taken a vacation or have taken them so seldom that it is hard to remember the last time they went on a trip.

In considering vacations, it is important to first understand what a vacation is. For most people, taking a vacation means that you are going to go somewhere for a specific amount of time. However, for some it doesn't mean that you have to travel anywhere. Just being at home with your spouse may be all you need to relax. It might mean just taking a break away from the distractions of work and the usual activities.

Taking a vacation with your spouse, or with your family, is an important ingredient as you nurture yourself, your spouse, your family, and your marriage. Vacations need to be done regularly and hopefully within your budget. They are times to rest your mind, to play, to enjoy one another's company without the distractions of daily living. It helps if you and your spouse have similar interests.

Evaluate: What You Enjoy Doing

When planning a vacation, take time to consider what your spouse wants to do. Ask yourself these questions:

1. When was the last time you took a vacation? _____

2. What was great about that vacation? _____

_____

3. What was not great about that vacation? _____

_____

4. What do you want to do for your next vacation? _____

_____

_____

5. What is your dream vacation? _____

_____

Now have your spouse answer these same questions.

1. When was the last time you took a vacation? _____

2. What was great about that vacation? _____

_____

3. What was not great about that vacation? _____

_____

4. What do you want to do for your next vacation? _____

_____

_____

5. What is your dream vacation? _____

_____

From the information you gathered regarding vacations:

- What does your next vacation look like? _____

  _____

- Where are you going? _____

  _____

- What are you going to do? _____

  _____

- When is it? _____

Over the years Reneé and I have enjoyed going on vacation with another family or with friends. We have formed a cruise club and have found it to be very enjoyable to travel with others.

Regular vacations will help you have a marriage that will last a lifetime. If you haven't been on a vacation in a while, it probably is time. Have a great time.

V – Vacations Are Important!

WEEDS CAN KILL A GARDEN

There are many reasons why a marriage dies. Here is a list of Marriage Killers – Weeds that need to be addressed.

Within this list are some reasons you may find it necessary to say, "I'm sorry." If you are guilty of any of these behaviors listed below, you may want to consider how to change the situation. If it is appropriate, you might consider confessing your fault, saying you are sorry, asking for forgiveness and then changing your ways. Some of these "killers" are not the result of anything you might have done; they are just part of life. Many of these patterns, if not changed, will be detrimental to your marriage and will increase the difficulty in attaining success. Most of these are very self-explanatory.

Possible Marriage Killers
1. Getting married too young
2. The death of a child
3. Being codependent
4. The way we lived in the past
5. The way we were raised
6. Our broken and unhealed self
7. Chronic illness
8. Lack of knowledge and understanding
9. Waiting too long to get help for your marriage
10. Not getting help at all
11. Generational patterns in your family

12. Over-commitment to your job or other activities

13. Unrealistic expectations

14. Being jealous

15. Having low self-esteem

16. Having an addiction problem

17. Pornography

18. Gambling

19. Sexual frustration

20. Loneliness

21. Infidelity

22. Business failure

23. Business success

24. Physical exhaustion

25. Excessive credit

26. Conflict over how money will be spent

27. Selfishness

28. Interfering in-laws

If any of these weeds are currently in your marriage, it is time to figure out a way that they will no longer have the ability to kill your marriage. One way to remove them is to begin using the principles we have already addressed. You can also find a mentor, spiritual leader, or counselor who can help you with these situations.

Evaluate: The Weeds in Your Marriage
Identify the weeds in your marriage that need to be addressed.

1. _____

2. _____

3. _____

And as always, ask your partner to make their list. Identify the weeds in your marriage that need to be addressed.

1. _____

2. _____

3. _____

Share the lists with one another and begin to get a plan to pull them out.

W – Weeds Can Kill a Garden!

X-RAY VISION IS HELPFUL

After going through *Webster's Dictionary* several times looking for an appropriate principle that will help you with your marriage that begins with X, it seemed quite obvious that what would be helpful would be the ability to see things that you can't see with just your normal eyes. I remember watching Superman and wishing that I could see through walls, that I could have X-ray vision.

What I have experienced in my marriage is that the better I know my spouse, the better I understand her, the better my marriage is. My ability to understand her, to see things even though they aren't obvious is increasing. My X-ray vision is improving as I gain more understanding.

We Just Don't Get It

Many times couples will come to see me and they will have offended or hurt one another, and they don't have a clue as to why their partner was offended. They just don't understand.

There are several areas that are common places where spouses hurt one another. For example, words that are said that are thought to be funny but are really sarcastic and judgmental are often hurtful. If we had clearer vision, the ability to see things that weren't obvious, we would not get in trouble because of the words that we speak. Another place where we hurt our spouses is when we forget special occasions, birthdays, anniversaries, and special holidays; like Valentine's Day, or Mother's Day.

We also cause hurt and misunderstanding when we flirt with another person at a party or a gathering. If you or your spouse is doing this behavior, it must disappear from your marriage. If you are at a party and abandon your spouse and let them fend for themselves, it will hurt them. It would be good if you had X-ray vision to be able to see the wound that was going to be caused by any of these actions.

There are many situations when it would be nice to see what was coming. I remember wondering how my mom knew what was going on all the time in our home when I was growing up. It was like she had eyes in the back of her head. Now that I am older I have begun to understand that she really didn't have eyes in the back of her head, or X-ray vision; rather, she had understanding. Some would call this being knowledgeable or having discernment.

This chapter is connected to the letter U regarding understanding. If you are to get better at knowing what is really going on and being able to increase your vision, you will have to take your eyes off yourself and begin to try to focus on what is important to your spouse. You will need to be looking toward them to see what they really need. You will need to try to understand what they are thinking. You will need to become less selfish and less self-centered. You can increase your vision.

Evaluate: How Are You Doing?

Take time to fill in the answers to these questions.

1. How am I am doing at understanding my husband or wife?_____

2. Where am I missing the mark? _____

Now ask your spouse to fill in the answers to these questions.

1. How is my spouse doing at being a husband or wife? _____

    _____

    _____

    _____

2. Where are they missing the mark? _____

    _____

    _____

    _____

Take what you have learned and begin to try to strengthen and nourish your marriage. With this newfound vision may you be able to see more clearly and be able to love more excellently.

X – X-ray Vision Is Helpful!

YOU THINK OF YOUR SPOUSE FIRST

In a marriage, there are many opportunities to think of your spouse first. You have had chocolate cake for supper and there is one piece left. Rather than devouring it yourself later in the evening, you ask them if they would like to have it. You get tickets to a concert, and one of the seats is behind a person with a big head obstructing your view. You ask your spouse which seat they would like to have.

You know that the dog needs to be walked and you volunteer to walk it, even though you walked it the night before. When you are doing your laundry, you have one more cupful of detergent; you ask them if they need any clothes washed before you wash yours. These are all practical ways to show your preference, your love for your spouse.

If you are the husband, opening a door and letting your wife enter first, or opening a car door for them is just standard operating procedure. You go out to eat and there is only one chair available while you are waiting to be seated. You offer it to your wife.

For the wife, you look to your husband, wanting to know his opinion and trusting him when he makes his decision to lead. These are very basic; however, they are practical illustrations of you thinking about your partner first.

It's Connected to Leadership

Thinking about your spouse first is directly connected to leadership and trust. In countless marriages when it comes to the question, "Who wears the pants?" or "Who's the boss?" the answer is often confusing. Often, the wife is looking for her husband to give leadership in the home, and the husband thinks that leadership is about control and domination. What she is looking for is leadership that is a shared partnership. What he is looking for is respect. In other words, to be considered first.

It is my opinion that the husband is to exercise leadership in his home. However, the leadership that I am describing creates order rather than chaos. It is not one person ruling over another, but rather two working together. It honors each other. It serves each other. It thinks of the other person first.

Decisions need to be made each day, and rather than just making them without consulting your partner, you communicate, find out their opinion regarding what needs to be done, and determine together what you are going to do.

How Can You Let Another Lead You?

Some wives are obviously afraid of letting their husbands lead. They have never seen leadership built around love, honor, and respect. It can be scary to place yourself under another's authority. If the wife is confident that her husband is a safe place, that in his heart are love and kindness, and he will think of her first, it will be easier for her to trust and be led.

In a healthy marriage, there are times when the wife exercises leadership by taking control, by taking charge. However, just as the husband is required to lead out of love, honor and respect, so is the wife required to lead in the same manner. The main principle is to think of your spouse first.

Two Basic Needs

In human beings there are two basic needs. The first need is **security**. Security is a convinced awareness of being unconditionally and totally loved without needing to change in order to win love. The second need is **significance**. Significance is a realization that I am engaged in a responsibility or job that is truly important and has a meaningful impact on another person.

Being able to trust her husband is necessary for a wife to feel secure. Knowing that the wife respects and trusts him helps him feel significant. The wife is confident that her husband will consider her opinion and think about her first. This settles her; it helps make her secure and know that she is significant. The husband is confident that his wife will respect and trust him. This encourages him and lets him know that he is significant in her eyes. This likewise settles him, he also feels secure.

Obviously, they are both tied together. It is important if we are to nurture our marriages that we are aware of both of these needs and purpose to make them a part of our love for our spouse. Thinking of your spouse first will help meet their needs.

Evaluate: Thinking of Your Spouse First

List three ways that you think of your partner first.

1. _____

_____

_____

_____

2. _____

_____

_____

_____

3. _____

_____

_____

_____

Ask your spouse if they feel you are preferring them — if they are feeling you think about them first. If their answer is no, ask them how you might begin to show them. This will involve you giving up being first. It will involve you serving them.

List three ways that your spouse thinks of you first.

1. _____

_____

_____

_____

2. _____

_____

_____

_____

3. _____

_____

_____

_____

If you can't think of three it is time to go to your spouse and have a conversation with them regarding them considering you first. As in the past, if you can do this without a third party helping you dialogue, go ahead and begin the conversation. If you need someone to help you, call them quickly and begin to enrich your marriage.

This is another building block that requires sacrifice on your part, but will yield a great return.

Y – You Think of Your Spouse First!

ZEST IS NOT JUST A BAR OF SOAP

We talked about romance being an important part of a marriage. I told you early on in this book that my hope was to help you increase romance in your marriage. Here is a final list of some suggestions that I believe can help increase romance in your relationship:

1. Call your partner to say, "I love you."
2. Listen to one another. (Keep your relationship growing.)
3. Take a bubble bath together.
4. Walk down memory lane.
5. Use new techniques for making love. (Liberate your attitudes.)
6. Reverse roles while making love.
7. Never use sex as a weapon or as a reward.
8. Take time with one another. Avoid hurry and fatigue.
9. Never compromise the dignity of your partner.
10. Keep your eyes open while you make love with your partner.
11. Never make fun of your partner or yourself.
12. Don't worry about the flaws of each other.
13. Don't judge yourself because of response problems.
14. Don't expect your partner to know what you like or don't like.
15. Be playful. (Be imaginative.)
16. Resolve accumulated hurts, resentments, and anger.
17. Talk to each other. (Discover what each of you enjoys.)
18. Allow yourself to receive pleasure.
19. Enjoy the romance of your present marriage stage.
20. Never forget how to laugh and be full of humor.

Marriage was designed to be exciting. It was designed to be fulfilling and great. Your marriage can improve. If it is in real trouble it can be helped. Don't give up.

Begin to practice the ABCs and hopefully you will see your marriage improve. Just like you learned how to read by putting the letters of the alphabet together, now you can begin to put together these principles. Applying them to your marriage will help you nurture and build up your marriage so that it will last your lifetime.

You might need to also ask God for help. He does work miracles.

Z – Zest Is Not Just a Bar of Soap!

PART III — ENCOURAGE

Looking Toward Tomorrow

MAKING YOUR MARRIAGE LAST A LIFETIME

Okay, take a big breath and relax. You've almost finished the book. Let's take a small peek into the future.

In order to help you formulate a plan, fill in the spaces below.

It seems to me that the first area of my marriage I would like to work on or focus on with my spouse is:

_____

_____

_____

Another area is:

_____

_____

_____

Now, share these with each other. Come to an agreement on one thing to work on first.

Make a plan, e.g., set an appointment when you will talk next, have a date, go through the conflict resolution steps on a specific issue. Write it down. Agree to get help if you get stuck.

Most people learn about marriage the hard way. They try something and if it doesn't work, they try something else. They may go get help from someone, but usually they just struggle along trying to figure out how to do marriage by themselves.

One way to continue to find help for your current situation is to take some time and reflect on what ABCs were a part of your home. Many of us learned what we know about being married from watching what went on in our homes as we grew up. In the following exercise identify what you learned in your home.

Evaluate: What Worked in Your Home?
Your life experience:

What ABCs were a part of your home?

1. _____

_____

2. _____

_____

3. _____

_____

What ABCs were missing?

1. _____

_____

2. _____

_____

3. _____

_____

If you feel like you have failed at your marriage, or at least several parts of it, and if you are now aware that many of the ABCs have not been a part of your relationship with your spouse, don't despair. Don't be discouraged. Don't be so hard on yourself.

It is time to begin anew. Give yourself another chance. Now that you have some very practical ways to help nurture and build your relationship, pick the one or two you identified as the places to begin and start giving it a try.

Stop: Red Light

You can bring great pain and frustration into your marriage when you try to make your spouse be what you think they should be, the perfect dream in your head. Stop trying to make them meet all your expectations and become someone they were never meant to be.

Look/Listen: Yellow Light

No one enjoys being married to a person who wants to change him or her into someone else, who wants to control their every thought and move in order that they will get their own way, or who complains and is disappointed about who they are, what they do, and how they do it.

Go: Green Light. Try Another Way!

There's a better way to view your spouse. Notice how you are alike. Also, notice how they are different from you. Different can be good. It helps take boredom out of your marriage.

Now is the time to treat your marriage partner the way you want to be treated. Most people like to be loved, cherished, appreciated, honored, and respected for who they are and for what they do.

Show your thankfulness and appreciation to your wife or husband for who they really are and for all they do for you daily. This is a great opportunity to continue to strengthen and nourish your marriage.

Remember, there are many different seasons of life in marriage: newlywed, first child, second child, moving, new job, losing a job, buying a house, five years married, ten years married, fifteen years married, twenty years married, children in elementary school, junior high, high school, college, married children, empty nest, grandchildren, retirement. You and your spouse are both changing and maturing the older you get. Neither you nor your spouse will be the same person five years from now.

The ABCs of Marriage can be referred to over and over in each season of your marriage to help you keep nurturing and building your marriage.

It is my sincere hope that the ABCs discussed will help you resolve and bypass frustration and tension in your marriage through the years. I also hope this helps you enjoy each other and your marriage even more. May your marriage last a lifetime.

Final Comments

My wife and I have been married over thirty years. I have tried to utilize every ABC in this book. They work. I know.

I am a Christian and believe that God helps people when they ask him. Over the years, many times, the only way that I could successfully attempt to live the ABCs is because I had help from God. He is able to give you wisdom if you ask Him.

May God bless you and help you.

— Tim Gustafson

THE ABCs OF MARRIAGE

The ABCs of Marriage, written by Tim Gustafson, is designed to help you: **Evaluate** your relationship, discovering where you are now, where you've been and where you hope to go; **Equip** you with tools, to help you and your spouse grow closer together and to help your marriage become stronger; and **Encourage** you with expectations of good things to come.

In this book are many questions for you to read and answer that will help you evaluate and reflect upon your family history, your past, your present marriage, along with future marriage goals. This book can be used before you marry and during any year of your marriage. It is a practical approach to help you work out several basic principles that will help you nurture and strengthen your marriage relationship. My hope is that this book will be an excellent tool for you, and one that you can give as a gift to others.

- -

Mail with check or money order to:
         GCCS, P.O. Box 70023, Overland Park, KS 66207

ORDER FORM

Number of books ordered _____	@ $17.99 per book	$_____
Sales tax *(for Kansas residents)*	@ $1.58 per book	$_____
Shipping and handling (mailed to your home)	@ $4.00 per order (1-3 books)	$_____
	@ $6.00 per order (4-10 books)	$_____
	TOTAL	$_____

Ship to:

Name _____

Address _____

City_____ State _____ Zip _____

To order by credit card, for bulk orders over 10 books, or for international orders, go to **www.gustafsonconsulting.org** or contact Leathers Publishing, 888-888-7696.